# *First Steps*

## To A
## *Physical Basis Of Concentration*

*An Initial Strategy For Parents And Teachers*
*Relating To Learning And Behaviour Problems*

**Roy Y. Anderson**

**Crown House Publishing Limited**

First published in the UK by

Crown House Publishing Limited
Crown Buildings
Bancyfelin
Carmarthen
Wales
SA33 5ND
UK
www.crownhouse.co.uk

First published 1999

**British Library Cataloguing-in-Publication Data**
A catalogue entry for this book is available from the British Library.

**ISBN 1899836349**

Printed and bound in Wales by
WBC Book Manufacturers,
Waterton Industrial Estate,
Bridgend, Mid Glamorgan.

# Table Of Contents

# List Of Figures

# Acknowledgments

Dr. Carl Delacato deserves much gratitude, for the essence of his thinking seems essential to set about establishing a physical basis of concentration where needed.

Also, my thanks go to Professor Dirk Bakker, Free University, Amsterdam; to Dr. Peter Blythe and Sally Goddard Blythe, Institute for Neuro-Physiological Psychology (INPP); to Julie Bradshaw, senior educational psychologist, Lancaster; to Sammy Clarke, deputy head teacher, Overton St. Helen's Primary School; to Sheila Dobey (INPP), Heriot Watt University; to Svea Gold, clinical educator and producer of educational television; to Dr. Susan Hallam, psychologist at the Institute of Education; to Dr. Kjeld Johansen, Baltic Dyslexia Research Lab; to Suzanne Naville, psychomotor therapist, Zurich; to Dr. Margaret Newton, Aston House Dyslexia Consultancy; to Mats Niklasson, Director of Vestibularis Centre, Sweden; to Rosemary Lee Porter, retired head of the Lancaster Reading and Language Service; to Anne Savan, teaching Science at Aberdare; to Alison Smith, head teacher, Overton St. Helen's Primary School; to Gwen Wilkinson (INPP), neuro-developmental therapist; to the 'photographic' model and his parents; and to the staff at Morecambe Public Library.

I am particularly grateful to Jane Field (INPP), neuro-developmental therapist, and to Fred Siddle, retired head of English at Morecambe Grammar School, who both provided unstinting assistance.

The INPP have made knowledge of strategies for SpLD more accessible through annual open conferences.

The views expressed in the book do not necessarily belong to anyone but the author.

# *Chapter One*

## The Problem Of Tiny Switch-Offs

Imagine how this man fared at school.

A 46-year-old welder in a shipyard was coached during an adult literacy campaign. After one year his reading age was rated at 7yrs 6m on a sentence reading test. Its first sentence, with words no longer than three letters, was dictated to him twice. Despite much repetition of phrases, he made five errors in both versions and omitted four words. All mistakes were different, so with 100% variability in ten errors it appeared difficult for him to keep his attention on the task.

A child with learning difficulties has to work hard at school even with the best of teaching, but more so if accompanied by poor concentration. His attention must be sustained enough to cope with the job in hand. Of course, everybody switches off occasionally. 'What was it I came upstairs for?' 'How do I spell that easy word(?) – my mind's gone blank.' We miss a bit of conversation in a moment's absent-mindedness, and even when we want to hear everything, it is not long before we miss some important detail. An air traffic controller said, 'As long as we have human beings in the system we shall have mistakes.' These switch-offs are not the end of our attention span, but only a sudden, short lowering of attention in the middle of what we are doing. Obviously, they are bound to interfere with learning if there are too many of these lapses.

### The Attention-Stretch

Although finishing a task in one attention span is good, completing a task unit (i.e. task-chunk) between two tiny switch-offs is vital. Consequently, the focus is on the time between brief switch-offs, which might be called the 'attention-stretch', and it should be long enough to allow a component sub-task to be completed without the interruption of a switch-off.

When a reader with concentration problems switches off at a familiar word, his automatic response is not engaged, so there is an 'easy word error' – the familiar word is 'easy' for him. For example, a word might be read correctly on one line but not on the next. Sometimes, switch-offs might also account for slips such as skipping a line or including a word from the line below. On less familiar words, a switch-off may not allow him to keep story clues and letter clues in balance, which results in a misclued error (a 'miscue') or refusal. However, we shall see that spelling offers a better measure of switch-offs and, also, if they are excessive we can reduce their number.

## The Basic Idea

The basic idea of the physical basis of concentration arises from the work of Dr. Carl Delacato (1959, 1963). He makes it clear that the later book, mostly on early motor development, is to be read in conjunction with the earlier book which deals more with sleeping. Delacato links sleeping with early motor development in a unified concept, but his work was criticised over 30 years ago for its undocumented claims and the extreme demands it placed on parents. Parent and professional associations combined to publish a statement to this effect (American Academy of Pediatrics, 1968).

The concept of devoting a few minutes of daily work to sort out the underlying reflexes was just not available at that time. The situation is quite different now. There is no need for any child who shows a severe concentration problem to spend long periods on early motor exercises. At the other end of the scale, there are many children in mainstream schools with only moderate concentration difficulties who can be greatly helped by a little time on exercises such as walking and crawling.

> **The vital idea which Delacato proposed in his works in 1959 and 1963 is that while the child grows, the sleeping, crawling and walking areas of the brain should develop. Ascending the brain stem, the successive areas should become strong and dominant in turn, forming a firm foundation for the development of the cortex. Language develops in one hemisphere, usually the left one, which should become dominant, while the other hemisphere becomes sub-dominant.**

This idea provides a simple initial strategy for improving a poor physical basis of concentration. If doing related exercises for a few minutes a day fails to bring satisfactory progress, that few minutes might be better spent on specialised modification of aberrant reflexes underlying both early motor development and the child's sleeping position. Certain work on listening and seeing also fits within the theory.

It should be simple to test the validity of this idea, applying it first to difficulties which involve poor concentration in children normally found in mainstream schools. The subjects should have an intelligence level between low-average and high to avoid any mental handicap masking the benefits, and should have no physical handicap which would make the exercises difficult. When the value of the idea has become established, it may then be used more readily with handicapped children, where their handicap allows. Had Delacato kept his studies entirely to mainstream children, the results would have been obvious. However, his early assistance of handicapped children did demonstrate his caring attitude.

To avoid complications, the common example of language ability residing in the left hemisphere is studied. The Montreal Neurological Institute found that, in the absence of early brain damage, over 95% of right-handers and about 70% of left-handers (Springer and Deutsch 1981) showed speech ability to be in the left hemisphere.

Exercises to improve the physical basis of concentration brings a new dimension to remedial work, and the benefits gained from the efforts are out of all proportion to the brief time taken to achieve them. The child is able to concentrate for long enough, so that previously unmanageable sub-tasks can be completed between switch-offs, because their attention-stretch is lengthened.

There does not seem to be a suggestion that the sub-dominant side has an opportunity to be strong and dominant before the language side. For the particular case of language dominance in the left hemisphere, the path in Figure 1 puts forward this possibility. However, the path should not be confused with the reticular activating system, a network of neurones also in the brain stem sending branches to all parts of the cortex. The network controls wakefulness and alertness but, according to the proposed theory, does not control the physical position which the body should tend to occupy when sleeping.

There is some evidence to support this order of development shown in Figure 1. We know that, in general, the left side of the brain controls the right side of the body, and vice versa. Babies have been observed reaching out first with the left hand, which supports the suggestion that the right hemisphere develops before the left hemisphere.

More importantly, Dirk Bakker says about reading, that the right hemisphere should develop perception of words before the linguistic left side takes over (Appendix 3). The right side sees words as a whole before the left side begins to use its greater analytical skills, and it seems that most teachers expect some useful sight words to be learnt before they begin to teach letters and word-building. So, it appears that the visuo-spatial side of the brain should have its chance to be dominant before the language side becomes dominant, and this idea proves to be a useful concept.

Figure 1 shows a child's development as a step-by-step path or flowchart. It may be useful to think of concentration as flowing in this way. It also helps if we think that the quantity of concentration gathered on the language side of the brain determines the extent of our ability to relate. For example, when we describe a person as 'with it' or '100% switched in', we can suppose that the bulk of his concentration is in the language hemisphere.

When someone switches off for a moment, we sometimes say he is day-dreaming, and this diagram gives us a way of thinking about that, too. It suggests that when we switch off for a moment or begin to doze we think in pictures. As we descend from relating (using the language side of the brain), we appear to proceed to the visual side of the brain, before possibly sinking to lower depths. Thus, we might ponder the possible path both of development and daily usage as shown in Figure 1.

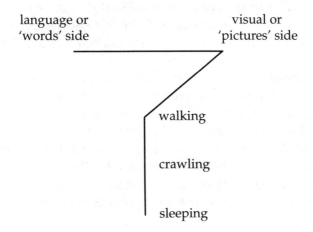

**Figure 1** *Path Showing the Brain's Suggested General Development of Concentration and Its Daily Usage*

'The more you look at it; the more you see in it,' said two people on different occasions about a similar diagram shown in Anderson's 'Helpful Ideas on Developing Concentration' (1977). One mother's enthusiasm was expressed as: 'I was sceptical when we first started this (sleeping, crawling and walking) but now I would recommend it to anyone.'

It is suggested that the flow-diagram is traversed up each morning and down each bedtime as the child's concentration-flow rises and falls, and it is also followed part of the way down from the words side when there are switch-offs.

If there is any weakness in the development of the brain in this manner, the child may not be able to sustain concentration on the 'words side' (left hemisphere) for long. The number of these switch-offs, big or small, could be excessive. Some of them may be almost imperceptible, but during a greater switch-off a child's attention might noticeably drift away and the child's gaze wander.

The idea is that concentration-flow ascends and develops levels of the brain-stem during the first year or so of life, and then primarily develops the right side of the brain before finally developing dominance of the left hemisphere at an average age of about eight years. Of course, advances of concentration-flow will be made early so that the language hemisphere will quickly show some signs of development, while the earlier stages are still being established.

These 'switch-offs' seem to be partly voluntary (as noted in Appendix 2), which is just as well for, otherwise, teachers would be wasting their time asking switched-off children to pay attention. However, much involuntary switching off can be greatly reduced. A powerful first step is to begin the day well rested so that the child makes fewer switch-off rest pauses when working. In practice, it is often weaknesses in the walking and crawling which draws the attention of parents in our first meeting.

## Early Motor Development with Sleeping

Delacato associates sleeping in the recommended position with the pons level of the brain-stem, i.e. the bridge between brain-stem and cerebellum. He stated in 1963: 'Children who are well organised at the level of pons, sleep on their stomachs in a homo-lateral position typical of the level of pons.' This statement means that the child whose neurological development is good sleeps in the well-known recovery position (also known as the relaxation position) shown in many first-aid books and in Figures 7 and 12. (Hopefully, the upper hand is kept under cover on cold nights!) The position is recommended for a child who can sleep in it, and it is the recommended morning rest position for any other child who has concentration problems and is physically able to use it.

Experience suggests that for practical purposes the child is fairly well organised if he stays in the recovery position for 20 minutes after falling asleep; is better organised if in the position for half an hour after falling asleep; and is best organised if he wakes up in it after appearing to stay in it, on one side or the other, all night.

Delacato regards cross-pattern creeping, which is our normal English crawling, as developing higher in the brain-stem at the mid-brain level (1963, 1966). In cross-pattern movement, arm and opposite leg move forward together. Higher still, he says that walking develops at the cortex level; apparently at the junction of brain-stem and cortex.

Delacato used homolateral crawling (English wriggling), with arm and leg on the same side coming forward together, but some followers have also used the cross-pattern wriggle, and the homologous wriggle with the four limbs pushing to the rear simultaneously.

The order of early motor movements introduced for children with moderate concentration problems is not so important as it is for reflexes when children have serious concentration problems. Each early motor movement seems to make a contribution, the work continuing until teacher and pupil no longer regard concentration as a problem, whereas the rule followed with reflexes is to progress systematically from the earliest weakness.

# Chapter Two

## Walking And Crawling

A check on brisk walking and crawling is an obvious starting point to see if Delacato-based theory is relevant to a child's poor concentration. Often improvement in attention is seen immediately after some practice in this area. There are a number of different movements involved in walking and crawling.

## Crawling

Svea Gold (1996) tells the story of a mother of five children who was concerned about the fourth child being hyperactive. Assume for the moment that overmuch switching off is involved, say by bringing a succession of stray topics back from the creative side of the brain to the relating side. The mother attended a lecture by Delacato, after which she spoke to him of her hyperactive son. He told the mother to crawl with the boy every day for 15 minutes, which she did, inventing wriggling and crawling games to assist the activity. Her son, however, became more wild. 'Then, on the twenty-second day, the child calmed down – and was never hyperactive again.' Also, the other children suddenly began to excel.

*What is the relevance of crawling?*
Dr. Carla Hannaford (1995) reports that 'infant crawling has long been known to be crucial for activating full sensory functioning and learning.' George Pavlidis (1981) noted that some dyslexics failed to crawl as children. Mats Niklasson, Director of 'Vestibularis', a Motor Development Centre in Monsteras, Sweden, says that 'a child who, even at ten years of age, learns to wriggle and crawl in a cross-pattern, might also cope better in class.' A cross-pattern movement involves diagonal pairs of limbs moving at a time, for example right arm and left leg. Gold (1986) advises a simple check on wriggling and crawling.

9

In an initial strategy for helping the child, there is something to be said for using the minimum amount of practice, so as to keep the child's maximum attention on an exercise. In addition to maintaining his interest, it leaves a memory of the exercise being done well. The latter was demonstrated to an audience when asked to write their names once and then three times; the first signature usually appeared neater. So, when a child's walking or crawling, for example, is found weak, he may be given a related exercise taking 30 to 90 seconds. The child is told to do exactly that each night until it is monitored the following week: a small number of such exercises give him a few minutes practice per session. This approach has helped many children aged 6 to 13 by easing learning difficulties until dominance is formed. (As a general rule, when a child loses concentration in a prolonged exercise or piece of homework, it is best to accept that his concentration span has ended and one should encourage him to stop.)

## Walking with Crawling

Weaknesses are often found in both walking and crawling. The earliest personal experience of work on these movements was with a boy of seven and a half years, one of several children withdrawn from class for remedial help. His teacher said, 'I can't do a thing with him,' and asked that he could be taken out every day even if others were left behind. He could not walk or crawl in the cross-pattern, so each day one of his tasks was to walk briskly 40 times across the classroom and crawl 40 times over a mat about 12 feet long. Within the week, the teacher exclaimed in the staff room: 'Oh! I can work with him now.'

Later, at a Remedial Reading Centre, two junior boys seemed to stop learning key sight words, words mostly taught before the child is ready for much phonics. The boys had each absorbed about 100 words from graded readers and related exercises. A check on their initial test records revealed that their crawling and walking were so bad that these had been stopped until help could be given. Once this was remedied, the two boys were learning words again within days.

Sam aged 8 yrs 4 m, tried to copy walking and crawling from television as a kind of play activity. Perhaps he felt an instinctive need for this, for he was found to be strongly homolateral in both progressions, his arm and leg on one side coming forward in unison.

## Walking

Sometimes walking has been tried on its own to see if it helps. Barbara Meister Vitale (1982) found that marching helped one junior boy's reading immediately. Another boy (8yrs 3m) was just beginning an exercise to form words by blending letters and could read the required letters. Surprisingly, he could not even blend 'a...d...ad'. He was asked to walk briskly across the room and back five times. After the walk, he sat down and hesitantly read the blend. Further down the page, he could not read 'b...ad...bad'. He said 'b...ad...bed' and stopped but, after repeating the walk, he slowly made the blend. Failing to blend gives an impression of how short the attention-stretch between switch-offs can be.

## Teaching the Walk

Walking in cross-pattern can feel difficult when thought about, as it often is when descending stairs. Therefore brisk walking is usually asked for to ensure conscious control. (One boy, of 11yrs 1m, seemed quite unable to do it at first.) Occasionally the child's walk may be slowed down for the same reason. The child will usually find space for a walk in the house of about ten steps, perhaps with a slight change in direction. Restricting him to four of these walks per session should maintain the useful improvement in attention.

When preparing for the walk, the body is erect and motionless, the feet are together with hands by the sides. In the test walk (Figure 2), the child is erect with eyes looking straight ahead and arms moving in parallel planes, whereas in the training walk (Figure 3) he looks down, directing the forward hand to point at the forward foot. At first, several test walks are performed to show up possible weaknesses; thereafter, training walks in each session may be accompanied by a test walk to observe remaining difficulties.

**Figure 2** *The Test Walk*

**Figure 3** *The Training Walk*

Watch the first step in particular, for it is important that both arms and the moving leg all begin in unison, and that the arms swing smoothly like a pendulum. Various irregularities might be seen:

1. Arm and leg on one side moving forward in unison.
2. Arms swinging forward together on the first step.
3. Arms swinging at a different rate to the legs.
4. Cross-pattern movement reverting to homolateral (as in 1.) after a few steps.
5. Dangling arms swinging only because of body movement.
6. Rear arm not swinging back at the first step as far as the other arm swings forward.
7. Putting one foot directly in front of the other, tending to make make the child topple.
8. Moving in jerky, or stilted, manner.

*(a) The Stilted Walk*

If brisk cross-pattern walking proves difficult, the child may be asked to copy a stilted walk. At the momentary pause, he points towards the forward foot with the opposite arm. Longer pauses between steps may be advisable at first, whereas shorter pauses may be used later for good conscious control of the limbs. The exercise prevents any hint of limp arms simply moving with the shoulders. On its own, this exercise appears to help the child begin to achieve both a cross-pattern movement and better blending, as the following case study shows.

A hard-working, co-operative girl supposedly of about average ability was in Year 3. Her reading age was nearly up to her real age, yet she could not blend. When asked to do a test walk, she tottered like a drunk. One stilted walk was demonstrated and at the next session (five weeks later, after Christmas) her stilted walk was satisfactory. She sat down and correctly blended five of a list of six phonic but uncommon three-letter words (e.g. 'wig, jot, led' rather than 'pat, dog, bed').

*(b) The Sitting-Crawl*

Another way of giving the feel of cross-pattern movement is by the sitting-crawl as shown in Figure 4, and described in Chapter 5. It teaches the idea of cross-pattern movement which is required to make balance possible in the crawl and walk, although these progressions often need a little further polish.

Two Year 3 boys at a rural school were struggling with regular three-letter blends. They were shown the sitting-crawl, which one did at home and the other did not. A week later, the first boy blended well, whereas the second continued to blend only some words correctly.

**Figure 4** *The Sitting-Crawl*

## The Crawl

When beginning the crawl shown in Figures 5 and 6, the arms are athletically straight; the hands are below the shoulders, opposite each other and shoulder width apart; and the fingers are pointing forward. Knees are opposite each other, thighs vertical, and forelegs and feet pointing to the rear. The feet stay on the floor in this movement and the back stays horizontal.

In Gold's 'When Children Invite Child Abuse' (1986), John Unruh's chart requires the head to turn to the outstretched hand and also that the eyes focus on it. Delacato (1963) firmly believes that this procedure is correct. It reflects the idea that crawling provides an important stage in the development of the baby's near vision, but, rightly or wrongly, experience related here has simply been with rhythm and co-ordination of limb movement.

**Figure 5** *Crawling Forward*

**Figure 6** *Crawling on the Spot*

Testing, daily practice and regular checks might each employ ten 'steps' on the spot; and, without breaking rhythm, moving forward for six steps. If the child's bedroom is small, crawling ten steps on the spot followed by one, two or three steps forward should, at least, teach and maintain the cross-pattern movement in that exercise, revealing and improving co-ordination that is not quite synchronized. Crawling on the spot is especially useful for the child who tends to lift one limb at a time when moving forward.

One of these weaknesses may manifest as:

1. Child rocking from side to side, lifting arm and leg on the same side together.
2. Movement becoming homolateral after a few steps.
3. Child's foot or feet rising from the floor when either mobile or stationary.
4. Hand and opposing knee not rising and falling in unison.
5. Child taking long steps as if trying to take most of the weight on his knees (request short steps for good balance).
6. Toes tucking under (toes should point to the rear).
7. Showing jerky movement.

If the child lifts his feet, he should be asked to drag them along the floor. 'For two weeks or so', mother held down the heel of her son (10yrs 10m) while he crept until that foot stopped rising involuntarily. The feet should also stay down in the stilted crawl, both on the spot and moving, in which the raised arm and knee hang for a moment, enabling the child to bring hand and knee down in unison.

One erratic and almost hyperactive boy (8yrs 3m) with limited application read to his mother after breakfast. When she had him do five minutes crawling just before reading, the mother felt that it 'definitely sharpened him up' and that he got through his reading much faster. Originally, he had had great difficulty placing his limbs correctly for this movement.

Students, too, it is reported, have been helped by a Baccalaureate for the University of Indianapolis Learning Disabled (BUILD) co-directed by Professors Nancy O'Dell and Patricia Cook. They believe that 75% of learning-disabled students (i.e. with specific learning difficulties) have an immature symmetric tonic neck reflex (see below) because they have not crept long enough as babies. So, those wishing to remain on the course must crawl for 15 minutes each day, five days a week. Inspired by Professor Miriam Bender's impressive results using only crawling, O'Dell and Cook now achieve a similar outcome; and in their book *Stopping Hyperactivity* (1997) provide crawling-related exercises for children assisted by parents.

The immature symmetric tonic neck reflex referred to above is an early reflex which must be eliminated not only to allow crawling to develop but to let the recommended sleeping and resting position become reflexive. It is dealt with in detail later in this book.

## The Cross-Crawl

Dr. Paul and Gail Dennison (1994) perfected and adapted the cross-crawl as a variety of movements where, 'when an arm moves, the leg on the opposite side of the body moves at the same time'. The cartoon of a figure walking on the spot is shown to say: 'It helps to touch the hand to the opposite knee occasionally to "cross the midline". When my brain hemispheres work together like this, I really feel open to learning new things.' Other exercises are given, which combine to form a 'Brain Gym' which they offer.

Hannaford in her book *Smart Moves* (1995) writes highly of the cross-crawl which for her is specifically walking on the spot with rising knee touching the opposite elbow. It 'should be performed very slowly', stimulating the balance mechanism. A bright 16-year-old boy certified as learning disabled did the exercise each morning and evening before bed. Within six weeks he was reading at his grade level and went on to gain a college degree in biology. The boy's clumsiness also improved, gaining him a place on the basketball team. Hannaford states: 'It took the Brain Gym activities to finally fit the pieces together.'

The two versions of the cross-crawl, 'hand to knee' like vigorous walking and 'elbow to knee' done slowly, deserve to be widely tried.

## Maintaining the Memory of Cross-Pattern Movement

When proficient in a movement, the child must do some repetitions of it each night to maintain its quality while signs of excessive switching off persist. The exercises might be stopped early, but if learning difficulties involving frequent switch-offs recur they should be resumed.

A significant quantity of cross-pattern walking may be needed to maintain the benefits that improved quality of walking can bring. Walking even short distances should help to firm the memory of cross-pattern rhythm in the cerebellum: a brisk walk of 100 yards/metres without stopping might need as much concentration from a child without hemispheric dominance as a mile or two does from someone who has gained dominance. The child can be reminded to swing his arms for a few steps near the beginning of each walk, which should encourage his arm-swing for the remainder of the walk.

If you are the parent of a child with weak concentration who really needs a lift to school, find an excuse for parking the car about 100 metres down the road. At least, he can then walk this last bit himself and repeat the procedure on the way home.

'After supper walk a mile' is well-known advice. Some cross-crawl is a good substitute if, at bedtime, the child feels too full of energy to sleep. The thumping which seems to be involved, however, would be better done on a floor with a firm foundation!

## Health and Hobby in Walking

Fortunately, walking is commonly rated as the most popular hobby of both men and women. The late Geoff Dyson, one-time AAA Chief Coach, was reported to have said that all athletes should do a two-mile walk each day whatever other training they do. It is possible that the cross-pattern rhythm is an important rhythm to be stored and retrieved from the cerebellum of a physically able child, and brisk walking seems the surest and simplest way of maintaining this store of rhythm.

# Chapter Three

## The Sleeping Work – 1. Introduction

The sleeping work has been welcomed by all the parents whose children with learning difficulties have tried it. Sleeping in the recovery position for about twenty minutes or more improves concentration.

Delacato stresses the importance of the position illustrated in Figures 7 and 12, saying that when children sleep on their stomachs the tonic neck reflex (tnr) is still present and that in his opinion its presence is a 'critical factor in ... language disabilities' (1959). 'We must ... preserve the integrity of the tonic neck reflex ... when we have the children sleep on their stomachs' (1963). Now, it is called the transformed tonic neck reflex (ttnr) position to distinguish it from the asymmetric tnr and the symmetric tnr.

### A Providential Coincidence

Over 25 years ago, children in mainstream education referred by an educational psychologist were coming to a Remedial Reading Centre. They had been doing small amounts of marching and crawling, but sleeping in the recovery position was part of their programme. It seemed a providential coincidence that possible switch-offs in reading were being studied at the same time that a form of sleeping work was introduced to all 50 children.

Each child was trained to turn from a certain position lying on one side to the same position on the other side. Many parents began checking their child after he fell asleep in bed every ten minutes or so to see if he was still in position. At the beginning, it was hoped that they could maintain half an hour in position.

A score based on the number of apparent switch-off errors made when reading a 100-word section of the child's class reading book was recorded in his homework book. '%N' meant neurological ability to stay switched on and not to switch off, judged by the child's performance in this 100-word passage. Examples of scores were: 100%N = no switch-off errors; 90%N = two switch-off errors; and 75%N = five switch-offs. No score less than 50%N was given. Not all errors were classified easily, but only an indication of switching off was required: for example, two consecutive slips, probably due to one slightly longer switch-off, were counted as one error at that time.

There often seemed to be some regularity to the switching-off and a number of children were recording five to ten unexpected errors in passages of 100 words. These were reduced to no more than two such mistakes when children slept in position for half an hour the night before. (Children good at walking and crawling, and who seemingly slept in position all night, still returned two easy word errors in 100 words.) Also, there appeared to be a relationship between the child's sleeping routine and his having a good learning day or not.

This relationship between time spent sleeping in the recovery position and the degree of switching off in the passage read the next day appeared to be significant, so it was checked for nearly a year. Teaching time was short, however, so only temporary records were kept.

Following the year's inquiry, a doctor's son of junior age was reading at the Centre without signs of excessive switching off. The impression was that he had slept in position for half an hour, but on reaching a long word he attacked it in a haphazard way, such as would normally be associated with one who had not slept in position for half an hour. Could he have slept well enough for the easy words but not well enough to tackle the harder words in an organised way? A suggestion was put in his notebook – '20 minutes in sleeping position, I think. Query!' As his mother came in to collect him from the Centre, she was asked how long he had slept in position the previous evening. 'Oh! Twenty minutes,' she said tentatively. Just afterwards, one written and several verbal affirmatives from parents via children agreed on 20 minutes for similar cases – not proof, but not contradictory either. Twenty minutes certainly seemed to be an easier objective for the children.

# Sleep and School Performance

One would expect sleeping to affect a child's school performance. This suspicion appears to have some foundation which varied examples suggest, although the effects of sleeping, walking and crawling cannot always be separated, as the following example clearly shows.

A 13-year-old girl at a Remedial Reading Centre was introduced to walking, crawling and sleeping in position. A very slow reader, she reported later that she might get all 'muddled' when reading, but after sleeping 'like that' she could read the book 'fine'. Also, the teacher at that Reading Centre reported years later that one of her parents was sure that the sleeping routine had benefited her son. Brian's head teacher said that they had tried everything without success for three years, but he had been 'got going' in a few months at the Reading Centre. The mother of another child said she was amazed that his (percentage N) score showed how well her son, an upper junior, had slept the night before. One father, a computer installer, twice claimed that the sleeping work was 'proved' to be successful.

The parents of Lucy, an upper junior at the Reading Centre, had come from Winchester, where they had heard about this approach. On one occasion, her mother said, 'When Lucy did not read well, I told her that she had not been in the sleeping position last night and the next night she tried to sleep in the sleeping position. The next day her reading was better. I definitely believe that when she has been in the position she reads better the next day.'

Clive (8yrs 4m), disadvantaged in home and housing estate, found it difficult to learn the sleeping-turn: his walk was strongly homo-lateral. During the next lesson at school, he seemed to come back more readily from his spells of being switched off, but these remained frequent. In a second home visit, he bent the wrong knee in the sleeping-turn; on the third visit in four weeks, his turn was satisfactory. The next week in school, he was surprisingly able to read, 'p-i-n...pin' – seven exclamation marks. He held up his arm and knee on one side, and after a moment said, 'I was in position all night'. Five days later, his teacher said that Clive knew 2 2s, 2 3s, 3 2s and 3 3s that day. When asked if that was good, he whispered, 'B..... marvellous'. That day, Clive was again 'good' at blending, but eventually he was placed in a residential school.

## Morning Rest in Position

There was a drawback, however, because sleeping in position was not within the full control of the child, but what seemed like a possible earlier step did give the child control: an energetic deputy head teacher said she lay awake in that position for 20 minutes in the morning to be fit for teaching. Another teacher, before becoming a deputy, said she lay in it for 15 minutes each morning for the same reason. Twenty minutes of this rest in the morning seemed to provide a benefit similar to the same time asleep in position the night before. Thus, in addition to all the common sense rules of going to bed, the sleeping work became lying awake in the recovery position for 20 minutes before rising; the child was also to lie in position for four to ten minutes – no more – trying to fall asleep in position at night.

This approach seemed to assist a remedial Year 3 girl on the first day that she succeeded in reading blends like 'e...d...ed, r...ed...red'. She had already claimed to have spent 20 minutes in the recovery position that morning. One parent, a bank teller, kept saying that she herself lay in that position for ten minutes on each side before rising. A more controlled testing of this work was needed, although continual evidence pointed to its value.

## An Investigation

An investigation was carried out (Anderson 1996) with 12-year-old identical twins, Adam and Bruce, both having a support teacher for specific learning difficulties (SpLD). They rested for 20 minutes, each in a different position – one on his back and the other in the recovery position. Variability of spelling was tested before and after this period. To maintain the co-operation of the children while resting, a story was read to them and amazingly just completed in twelve sessions of 20 minutes each. (Sleeping position and position on the floor were swapped equally in each block of four sessions.)

Whichever way the average scores were examined, lying in the recovery position, rather than on the back, had a worse effect on variability of spelling. This fact suggested that the ability to listen to a story was in conflict with the onset of drowsiness resulting in a more fatigued brain taking the second variability test. One can deduce that the recovery position tends to rest the brain more than does lying on the back.

## A Comparison

Compare the times with those of Dr. Kjeld V. Johansen (1993) who shows a graph of 'brainwave activity in a young man ("in his early twenties, lying with his eyes closed – but not asleep" adds Johansen) before and while listening to music designed to dampen hyperactivity and to release stress.' The graph 'after 15–18 minutes of listening' is clearly the regular, relatively slow beat of the alpha rhythm, which is the brainwave regarded as indicating relaxation.

If this experience is comparable, 20 minutes rest in the recovery (relaxation) position before rising might usually establish the alpha rhythm. This rhythm may release feelings of stress in the brain, allowing the person to begin work feeling fresh, and maintain some benefit for much of the day. Fifteen minutes resting in the sleeping position might be too short to recommend as a target.

## Waking in Position

Of course, if a child wakes up in position there should be no need for relaxing like that in the morning; the brain should be rested well enough, provided things such as bedtime and health are satisfactory.

Such seemed to be the case one day with William (Year 3) whose mother had him spend the requisite time in position each morning; she was delighted that he was 'better' in the mornings and was even willing to tackle his homework in the evenings. At 7yrs 11m, William had one of his best days, which turned out to be the first day that William was seen to wake in position.

## Feeling Fresh on Waking

Experience leads one to expect a child to feel refreshed on waking, and some examples illustrate this freshening. Adam (10yrs 7m), later statemented for SpLD, claimed to fall asleep in position four nights in the first week. Mum was taken aback on the second or third morning: on arriving at the breakfast table, he stretched his arms and exclaimed that he felt 'really refreshed' (see Anderson 1996, 1997).

A top junior girl reported a similar feeling. Her father was a lorry driver who rose at four o'clock in the morning, and woke the family as he was leaving the house at five o'clock. Normally the girl got up, put a shirt on and popped back into bed for she was tired. After she began to fall asleep in position, she felt fresh enough to stay up after her father roused her.

When neighbours paid a visit, the oldest child (6yrs 1m) of three was taught the sleeping-turn, which he picked up quickly. That night he fell asleep in position and was found in it half an hour later, but not after two hours. Next morning he was the widest awake and liveliest, which surprised them.

## Willing to Go to Bed

Persuading children to go to bed may not be such a struggle either. Two brothers of junior school age, friends of the family, were taught the sleeping position. They had not been keen to go to bed, but Mum was happy to report a new willingness. Several children have reported that having learnt the new position they could not thereafter sleep in any other way, and a few have volunteered that they were sleeping better.

Attending a college lecture on this idea, one secondary school year-tutor observed that the sleeping, crawling and walking helped to create a bond between parents and child when other methods failed to do so. Even a parent who is illiterate can co-operate with their child in this work.

The benefits of the sleeping work simply become accepted as normal; one expects them. Factors like illness and excitement appear responsible for the occasional ineffectiveness. However, the impression has been gained that failure to carry out this sleeping is the commonest cause of mainstream children with weak concentration having bad learning days.

The sleeping assignment is not much to ask of a child and should be made available to children with learning difficulties which are aggravated by poor concentration. If maintaining attention again becomes a considerable problem, the first question to ask is, 'Has the sleeping work been given up?' The sleeping routine appears basic and so of high priority. In simple terms, you cannot perform at your best if you have not rested well, and the recovery position serves this purpose.

# Chapter Four

## The Sleeping Work – 2. Making A Start

### Teaching the Child

To begin with, the child practices turning over on his front from one side to the other – the sleeping turn – on the carpet. He can move legs, arms and head to the count of five, until the turn becomes one movement. Beginning in the recovery position (Figure 7), he proceeds as follows:

1.  Pushes down the bent leg (Figure 8).
2.  Pushes down the bent arm (Figure 9).
3.  Turns the head to the other side, keeping on the front (Figure 10).
4.  Bends the other arm up (Figure 11).
5.  Draws up the other knee (Figure 12).

When proficient, the child is asked to lie in position for 20 minutes each morning before getting up.

The child should be encouraged to lie in position for two minutes on each side when he settles to sleep, beginning with the less comfortable side. A junior girl said she counted up to 119 before turning out of position – about two minutes. A Year 6 girl said (screwing up her face) that five minutes on one side felt 'weird', but added that she could manage two minutes – even three. After becoming used to the sleeping position, however, children often appear able to lie for five minutes in position on each side at bedtime. The routine is followed each evening until the child falls asleep in position.

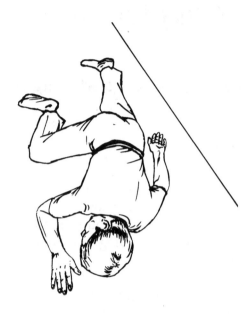

**Figure 7**   (Begins in the recovery position.)

**Figure 8**   (Pushes down the bent leg.)

**Figure 9**   (Pushes down the bent arm.)

**Figure 10**   (Turns the head to the other side.)

**Figure 11**   (Bends the other arm up.)

**Figure 12**   (Draws up the other knee.)

Occasionally, a child reports lying ten minutes on each side, which is unwise. If he does not fall asleep within ten minutes (or five on each side) he should return to his usual position; he may become too soporific to bother moving. This problem was seen with one girl (11yrs 0m) who was lying in position for perhaps 1½ hours she thought, not bored but not asleep either. Obviously the 'ten minute' warning should be heeded.

A person sleeping in this position needs only one thin pillow which reduces draughts and is usually more comfortable than none. It might be a good thing if the pillow is placed so that the sleeper's nose is off the edge.

The child may sleep on either side. One child, having learnt to fall asleep in position, was surprised to awake one morning in position but facing the other way. Another child said he realised at lunch-time that he had woken up in position but was facing the other way. Delacato tells us that 'The child who is well developed at this stage usually moves from one of these (left-sided or right-sided) positions to the other throughout the night' (1982). There must be many people who sleep all night in the recovery/ relaxation position, like one primary school head teacher whose dynamic energy may have been a consequence. (Some people claim at first to lie in position but do not have the lower arm completely behind the body.) Yet, do they appreciate the benefits? It can only be at changing over from an inferior position that one can appreciate the advantages.

## Bedtimes

Watching exciting television in the half-hour before settling cannot rest the brain ready for sleep, so if a set is allowed in a child's bedroom its viewing should be monitored.

Also, studying late in the evening may make it hard for a child to sleep. One day William (7yrs 11m) was looking around, matching his cards far from systematically and was generally dozy. Mother was surprised, for she reported he had again woken in position. She, however, had been doing school work with him till late the evening before, and subsequently he had had a restless night. It is wise to choose a sensible time beyond which the child is not allowed to study.

On Fridays and Saturdays, staying up half an hour extra is probably enough, even though friends might be staying up much longer. Children showing an excessive number of switch-off rest pauses appear to take longer than usual to recover from a late bedtime, and to regain a satisfactory level of attention in lessons.

Michael, a clumsy (i.e. dyspraxic) child nearing 11 years of age, offered the greatest tendency in one school to produce bizarre spellings. He was learning to organise his ways of spelling, but in one session was quite confused. Seen weekly, on Monday mornings, Michael could in no way make an orderly response that day. Bedtime, normally 9.00 p.m., had been 10.30 on Friday evening because his scout meeting had been followed by supper with a TV programme: he stayed up till 10.30 again on Saturday, so an urgent plea was sent home. The next week Michael's spelling was only slightly better: bedtimes were reported to have been 10.20 on Friday, 9.30 Saturday and the usual on Sunday. The following week his spelling was about normal, reporting bedtimes of 9.45 Friday and 9.15 Saturday. In mid-secondary school, the Centre for Developmental Learning Difficulties helped Michael's aberrant reflexes and his mother, who was not easily satisfied, was pleased to be shown improved movement at each session of monitoring.

Another example was Joseph, who was nearly ten years old when he began the sleeping work; a normal bedtime was reported to be 8.30 p.m. On the second Monday morning session after beginning the regime, he was sure he had stayed in position for 20 minutes before rising, yet he was dozy as usual. On the telephone, his father explained that Joseph's grandparents had let him stay up till 10.00 on Saturday, which seemed to be the problem.

Superfluous energy might cause a restless night. 'After supper walk a mile' may not always be practical, but, as a last resort, some exercise can take the edge off excess liveliness. The exercise might well include a cross-crawl, especially if cross-pattern movement is weak and dominance is not established.

## Assistance by Parents

One mother told her son, while he was asleep, to turn over into the sleeping position. He did so but, in the morning, could not remember it. On the other hand, one mother concentrated so much on putting her son in position after he was asleep that he forgot how to get in it by himself. If either is considered necessary, the first method seems preferable; but the junior child's sleeping-turn should be checked occasionally, for sometimes the young ones do forget it.

One boy went to bed regularly at nine o'clock, and mother said that she usually checked his position at quarter past. He was relatively easy to put in position, normally keeping in it for the desired half-hour. She, however, sometimes got 'stuck' on a job and did not check his position until just before the news at ten o'clock. Then it was much harder to put him in position and he did not usually stay in it for half an hour. If such intervention seems necessary, it probably should be given sooner rather than later.

The 'amazed' parent, referred to earlier, also claimed on another occasion that her son had slept in position for half an hour. It was suggested to her that she might be mistaken because of the great number of switch-off errors in reading. 'Oh! But I put him in position every 15 minutes,' she responded. It was explained to her that he had to stay in it for the half-hour. If he came out of position after a few minutes -, she should give it up that evening, for he would probably keep doing so.

Expectant mothers who are taught at antenatal clinics to sleep in the relaxation/recovery position are well able to teach their older children this sleeping position. As stated, the recommended position is also named the transformed tonic neck reflex (ttnr), which usually appears at about eight months (see Chapter 11). It is wise, therefore, not to put a child in position in the first year; and, when it is done, he must be able to turn onto his back if too hot in bed. It may be best to wait until he is old enough to be persuaded to try it.

## Troubleshooting

One girl proclaimed the position was uncomfortable but, when she demonstrated it, she was lying on her arm rather than having it behind her. The position was re-learnt. A boy found the position hurt his rear arm, which was obviously because he was bending it with the elbow nearly at shoulder level, a practice soon corrected. A lively girl complained of waking up when she turned in the middle of the night. When her sleeping-turn was checked, it was found to be energetic, but complaints ceased after it was slowed.

One junior girl (possibly 8 years old) generally slept in position on her left side but sucked her right thumb. Her dummy had been stood on at an early age and she had rejected the replacement. Turning over, she slept on her right shoulder with the same thumb still in her mouth. This turn, of course, altered the sleeping position, so she was asked to sleep on her left as much as possible.

## General Value

Parents and camp leaders who tell their children to 'turn over and go to sleep' know they settle to sleep better this way than on their backs. The recovery position is particularly useful for lulling the mind to sleep when one is accustomed to it: one prospective mother learnt it so quickly at the antenatal clinic that she had to be woken when the lights were turned up. The position is useful for the whole family. Coaching of private pupils having finished at one home, mother ended with, '...and thanks for teaching us good habits – the sleeping, you know.'

It is best if a person can sleep through the night in position either on one side or the other. Should anyone wish to stay asleep in position but be unable to do so, it seems like a worthwhile objective for specialist work on the underlying reflexes.

Adults may not all choose to sleep or rest in this way, but our children with problems involving poor concentration need all the assistance they can acquire to be fresh for lessons the next day.

# Chapter Five

## Rhythm And Rest Pauses

Work done in rhythm tends to channel the switch-off rest pauses between task-chunks which are, in consequence, not so frequently 'hit' by the switch-offs. Rhythmic work contrasts with work done in sudden rushes which tend to overload the brain and disrupt these sub-tasks.

Whereas adequate rest at night reduces the apparent need for rest pauses when learning, rhythm tends to organise them to cause less interference with tasks. Rest is mostly done at home while school employs rhythm.

### The Early Development of Rhythm

The Channel 4 television programme 'Equinox' (20-11-94) reported the startling benefits of exposing an unborn child to rhythm and music. Dr. Brent Logan of Oregon played variations of a synthesised heartbeat for a foetus, and Dr. Mikhail Lazarev of Moscow played a course of musical training. The booklet accompanying the programme, 'Brave New Babies: Learning Before Birth', gives further details.

A child's sense of rhythm develops early in life, and many rhythmical movements have been observed in the first year. Among the early progressions, the rhythm of walking might have the greatest impact, partly because so much of it is done. Early motor movement appears to be learnt primarily in the brain-stem, which has connections with the cerebellum, where the rhythm is almost certainly memorised. Later, in school, rhythm is seen to help the child in many ways.

## Rhythm in Reading and Writing

In the early stages of teaching, an adult may read part of the text with the child. (The length of section, and overlapping of reading **to, with** and **by** a child depend on the text difficulty – eventually he just reads **by** himself.) Helper and child co-operate in selecting phrase lengths to govern the rhythm of pausing. Reading together not only organises sentence breaks by meaning but also serves to keep the readers in unison, which teaches the child phrasing and, with it, rhythm. Thus, momentary switch-off rest pauses are more readily channelled between phrases.

In cursive handwriting, the word becomes the unit of rhythmic work, with switch-off rest pauses channelled between. Of course switch-offs do not occur between all words. Nevertheless, when one does happen it is more likely to be as the pen or pencil rises from the end of a word, which invites a momentary rest pause if the brain is ready for one.

## Changes of Pace and Attention

Obviously, it is important to work at a suitable pace. The rhythm of an activity normally slows when heightened awareness is required, such as while emerging from a new car in a tight garage. There might also be a momentary pause as, for example, before knocking on a VIP's door, giving instructions, or switching off the computer. Children with SpLD (specific learning difficulties), in particular, should be taught the need for appropriate changes of pace and attention.

On the other hand, an error, say in writing, should not be corrected with a rush to keep up the average speed, for it may encourage a switch-off. Instead, the child should accept that the error has caused a delay, and the correction should be made without much change of pace.

## Cursive Writing Promotes Dominance

At about the time that the junior child's handwriting becomes uniformly neat, there often occurs that sudden widespread progress probably indicating the gain of dominance. (For a few children, a particular ability or disability in handwriting means that its improvement does not come at the general surge.) Better cursive handwriting probably facilitates the normal development of dominance by channelling rest pauses. For this reason, the child is asked to produce very neat handwriting for a time until that sudden increase in all-round ability and ability to learn. Subsequently, he may revert to handwriting which simply responds to the needs of the moment. This style might often be near-cursive writing with the pen frequently flying over the paper without the suggestion of a switch-off.

If the child's style is being changed from print to cursive, he should be asked to practise newly taught letters in his creative writing. The child should not have to hold back until all letters have been taught before using them, because he should be putting into practice what he has learnt. Thus his writing is a temporary mixture of print and cursive, for which the teacher should prepare the parents. On the other hand, if cursive is taught from the beginner's class, a constant watch must be kept to avoid the awkward forming of letters becoming a habit and storing up a dreadful problem for a remedial group later on.

## Early Motor Development Assists Blending

Some children find particular difficulty in correctly combining the sounds of three-letter words of the kind you can sound out. A little work aimed at increasing the attention-stretch nearly always solves the problem. It seems that the child can switch off in the middle of a sub-task from the words side of the brain to the pictures side, and experience disorder; or he can switch back in again and forget something.

For example, he might sound out 'c...a...t ... (switch off) ... dog', making a reversal (more on this subject later) or a confusion. On the other hand, after saying 'c...a...t', he might switch off and back in again; coming out with, say, 'cot', having forgotten the vowel. In either case the attention-stretch is not long enough to complete the blend.

As well as helping to establish other cross-pattern movements if necessary, the sitting-crawl should nearly always be enough to deal with delayed ability to blend. In the exercises, the child can give more attention to the cross-pattern co-ordination because the body is supported, and he cannot switch off easily during the exercise due to the chosen timing. The following section is taken from Anderson (1983), with thanks to the National Association of Special Educational Needs, with some modification.

## The Sitting-Crawl

While remedial juniors and top infants were learning their letter sounds, another part of their work was to learn aural blending of regular three letter words in stages. For example: 1. win-dow, 2. ch-air, 3. w-all, 4. a-t, 5. f-a-t, with about one second between word parts presented. Some children, nevertheless, just could not cope with level 5.

It appears that we can specify one effect of this piece of early motor development (emd). Under normal conditions referred to below, it seems that perfecting the sitting-crawl enables almost all of these non-blending children to blend.

The idea of strengthening the brain-stem led to trying the sitting-crawl with a child who could not blend regular three-letter words aurally received. He blended correctly after perfecting the exercise in the way described below.

With the first ten or so children who were assisted in this way, only one failure was observed. Since then, there were no failures with an estimated fifteen or more other children about that time (and with many others since). Furthermore, and more importantly, no regression has been suspected.

With regard to the one 'failure', it appears likely that background factors such as tiredness, lack of motivation and the beginning or ending of illness could have been responsible. Indeed, the high degree of success has been surprising. Only short attention-stretches, however, are required for the child to stay switched in for regular three-letter blends whether presented orally or visually.

The procedure used for teaching the 'sitting-crawl' is as follows. Each stage is attempted only when the previous one has been well learnt. All limb movements are performed smartly and at the moment when the number is spoken.

## Stage 1

The child sits comfortably with feet resting on the floor while his hands lightly hold the front edge of the chair. He counts from one to six in approximately four seconds and at an even rate. The child lifts one hand at the count of two, keeps it still on the count of three, and lowers it on the count of four. Hands and feet are kept down on the count of five and six, which breaks the automatic up-down-up-down response; often it seems that the limbs want to keep moving in a regular rhythm of their own. The count demands good conscious control. The raising and lowering is not in a wave motion but in crisp movements: still, up, still, down, still, still.

The count of six is used as the child lifts and lowers –
(a)   one hand slightly five times,
(b)   the other hand five times,
(c)   one knee slightly five times,
(d)   the other knee five times.

This exercise is demonstrated to the child, who then copies it. Once a day at home, the child does only that amount to ensure he maintains full attention. Progress is normally seen when the child's ability is monitored at the end of the week. Improvements appear to show how faithfully practice has been done.

## Stage 2

The same count of six is used as the child lifts and lowers –
(a)     one hand and the opposite knee together five times,
(b)     the other hand and other knee in unison five times.

Again, all limbs stay down on the count of 'five' and 'six'. As expertise develops, the teacher keeps the lesson short (about one minute) in order to show the child how to limit his practice session.

## Stage 3

The count of six is used as the child lifts and lowers –
(a)     one hand and the opposite knee together three times,
(b)     the other pair of limbs in unison three times,
(c)     the first pair three times,
(d)     the second pair three times.

It is the change from one pair of limbs to the other pair which is clearly more difficult. There was one change per session in stage 2, whereas in this stage there are three.

## Stage 3a

Occasionally this in-between stage is needed before stage 4. It is the same as stage 3 except 'three times' is replaced by 'two times'.

## Stage 4

This stage is the same as stage 3, but each co-ordinated 'step' of one hand and the opposite knee alternates with a step of the other pair of limbs. This movement is the requisite cross-pattern step, though stilted. The child is asked to do ten to twenty such steps daily until conscious control of the stilted action is good, each movement synchronised to the count.

When stage 4 is mastered and when the child is considered to be physically well, emotionally stable and reasonably well rested, his ability to blend is re-tested. (Progress in blending cannot be expected at earlier stages.) Newly successful blending probably indicates a slightly improved attention-stretch with easing of learning difficulties.

The child is asked to continue with four to ten steps each day until he is sure of his blending. It is probably best done just before bed because it seems to promote sleep for children who need the exercise (Chapter 12). All in all, this exercise has proved to be very useful.

### Early Movements

Work done so far might reduce frustration enough to satisfy teacher and learner. On the other hand, for a particular child, it might appear wise to tackle his weaknesses in the early movements of wriggling, rolling and bicycling.

### 1. The Cross-Pattern (or Army) Wriggle

In the army wriggle (Figure 13), the arm and opposite leg come forward together while the other two limbs propel the body. The body is resting on a support as in the sitting-crawl, which might be used to improve this cross-pattern movement if difficult.

### 2. The Homolateral Wriggle

The arm and the leg on the same side come forward together in the homolateral wriggle, which is begun with the child lying in the recovery position. Delacato (1963) states that 'We find that a daily five-minute period of homolateral crawling (i.e. English wriggling) is usually sufficient to establish a proper sleep position in children with normal mobility, in four to eight weeks.' Although the need for a polished surface poses difficulties, the next and associated exercise might be suitable for an initial strategy.

**Figure 13** *The Army Wriggle*

## 2a. The Repeated Sleeping-Turn

The repeated sleeping-turn is the stationary form of the homolateral wriggle, which Delacato considers almost as effective as the mobile form. More experience of this exercise might be profitable.

## 3. The Homologous (Swimming or Frog) Wriggle

Upper juniors are usually happy to tackle this wriggle (Figures 14 and 15). Delacato's work was done some years ago at a school in Winchester, for children who would now be considered to have 'moderate learning difficulties' (an IQ of just below the wide 'average' band). The teacher considered the frog wriggle important because several times it had appeared to produce a surge of learning.

**Figure 14** *The Frog Wriggle: Before Step*

**Figure 15** *The Frog Wriggle: After Step*

Perhaps the exercise helped to bring the symmetric tonic neck reflex under conscious control, allowing the transformed tonic neck reflex (ttnr) to be better established. If so, the child would then possibly be better able to stay in the ttnr (recovery) position all night.

Lying prone and keeping symmetrical, the hands are placed a few inches in front of the shoulders with fingers pointing forward. The elbows and, to some extent, the knees point out to the side, with feet remaining in line with the buttocks. Toes bend under and try to grip the floor. The four limbs push back in unison, levering the body forward a few inches on each step. If it is expedient to allow shoes to remain on; those with flexible soles are best.

Co-ordination is probably more important than length of step. A number of children tend to pull with the arms only or to push with just one leg. Holding the child's heels might be necessary. Another useful idea is to ask the child to stand, splay knees out, and practice springing up. Children usually improve their performance by doing three or four 'steps' per day using maximum concentration.

Some children in mainstream education are weak at the earlier levels of bicycling and rolling. The severity of the concentration problem or, possibly, the early motor difficulties might determine whether to go this far with a child, but usually the movements can easily be improved.

## 4. Rolling

Smooth co-ordination is the aim in a rolling exercise, and some mainstream children have difficulty controlling the knee movement. The child lies on his front with hands by his shoulders and begins to roll smoothly. By the quarter turn, his knees are drawn up until his thighs make about a right-angle with his body. After nearly a full turn, the child straightens his legs, preparing to reach the original prone position. However, the reader might also refer to a test of the 'segmental rolling reflex' in Field 1995 and Goddard 1996.

## 5. Bicycling

This bicycling exercise aims to help with another possible weakness in early motor development. The child lies on his back with knees and elbows bent. His fists are just above his shoulders and his feet are off the ground. Fists and feet move in nearly circular paths in vertical planes, a movement which is difficult for some mainstream children. Separately, the foot movement can be practised while sitting, and the fists rotated while standing in front of a mirror.

Some authorities consider it helps the child to brachiate, which means swinging along from hand to hand under a horizontal ladder, a bit like a monkey. It can be rationalised that the movement fits in with evolutionary development and so with early motor development. Most parents, however, would find it too inconvenient as part of an initial strategy.

Perhaps the final word should come from Australia. ANSUA Children's Learning and Development Centre, P.O. Box 11, Paddington, Queensland 4064, believes in the importance of a wealth of movement experiences from birth. In their Newsletter (March 1992), Jean Rigby writes: 'It is said that in order to develop well a child needs 1000 hours on the floor before he walks. Our society tends to prevent this through the use of bouncinettes, baby-walkers etc. ...'

# Chapter Six

## Gaining Hemispheric Dominance

### The Basic Idea

The idea of hemispheric dominance is that one side of the brain rules language and movement. Samuel Orton (1937) blamed a lack of some one-sided superiority for problems in language development.

Dr. Margaret Newton (1970) used electroencephalograph studies to note alpha activity, which are brainwaves associated with resting. She found more of it in the non-dominant hemisphere of the 25 controls (i.e. children as normal as possible, each one matched to a child in the experimental group), but with no such difference in hemispheric activity in the 25 dyslexic children (mean reading ages 10.3 and 6.4 years respectively). The control group seemed to have 'a lateral dominance', but the dyslexics showed 'no comparable resolution of dominance'.

Hemispheric dominance is a more accurate term than cerebral dominance, which is also used, but the terms are often shortened to dominance. The approach suggested in this book should bring forward the acquisition of dominance, with a consequent reduced frustration in learning.

### Reversals and Confusions when Switched Off

Many years ago, it was suggested that the symmetry of the two hemispheres of the brain would result in a visual image in one hemisphere causing a mirror image in the other (Orton 1925). Although the idea has been controversial, Richard Masland, Professor Emeritus of Neurology, Columbia (1981), refers to later support for it in both experiment and theory. For example, Nancy Mello (1966) gives the interesting case of the pigeon, in which each eye transmits only to the opposite hemisphere. Nearly all of her pigeons trained on left-right mirror-image problems with one eye blindfolded showed reversals when tested with the other eye.

Orton (1937) drew attention to the instability of this reversal tendency in reading. Perhaps what is happening is that sometimes the child is switched in to the dominant hemisphere, but sometimes is responding primarily from the other side of the brain (with all the brain co-operating, of course). Regular switching off might sometimes be suspected, as noted in Chapter 3, but usually one would expect the child's reversing to be unpredictable.

Switching off from the language side to the less orderly side of the brain will undoubtedly produce confusions as well as reversals; so both may occur in the momentary switch-offs.

## Concentration-Flow

One highly rated educational psychologist said that he could not 'think that way' about the developmental idea suggested. It seemed that something else was needed. Now, someone had written that eventually we might have to think of concentration as flowing. The concept of concentration-flow helps us to appreciate the basic idea, for it is convenient to think of a switch-off as 'concentration' flowing briefly from the language side of the brain to the other side. Momentarily, the smooth working of the dominant hemisphere is opposed by the less organised side of the brain; the language of the better-relating side is fleetingly ineffective.

When concentration is considered to flow from the words side to the pictures side of the brain (Figure 1), it must appear to be going downhill, in effect. This idea fits with the idea of a reader lost in his own visual world when reading a light novel at bedtime: concentration is already sinking from the relating side to the pictures side as a precursor of sleep.

The left hemisphere appears to need concentration to be at a higher level than does the right hemisphere. For example, old people who find it hard to maintain concentration on the language side can often continue to enjoy handicrafts using the creative side. Also, when a person day-dreams, we can think of his concentration flow 'sliding down' to the visual side.

If there is any discomfort, a person may slide down from what is normally the relating side to the more self-absorbed, poorly relating side of the brain, with excessive, momentary switching off or a series of wilfully extended switch-offs. These could play havoc with a child who has SpLD.

A child's concentration is on the language side of the brain when he is answering questions; responding to input, he is on the relating side of the brain. On the other hand, the more self-centred side of the brain might give rise to a monologue as, perhaps, with the child in the following case study.

A boy with an IQ of 118, actual age 7 yrs 6m, progressed from 6yrs 10m to 8yrs 5m on a word recognition test with six sessions over five weeks – perhaps due to a gain in hemispheric dominance. Shortly after beginning the sleeping work, his mother commented on his improved handwriting, a willingness to correct a hand-writing error and 'less babbling in his conversation'. This babbling may have been irrelevant and disorganised speech, but still under-standable, with stray topics coming to the language side of the brain from the pictures/creative side. However, inarticulate babbling might have been initiated at a lower level (see Figure 1).

## The Establishment of Hemispheric Dominance

Adults, if free from stress, are normally more comfortable when usefully employed than children are. On the other hand, children hate what they label as 'work'; probably, in part, because they keep switching off, losing the thread of their thought. At an early stage of development, a child's switching off obviously is considerable, whereas it is not normally much with an adult.

As the child grows there should come a time when he stops frequent switching off. It is the point of achieving hemispheric dominance when he can keep his concentration mostly on the relating side of the brain. Many things such as organisation, spelling, handwriting, and other skills in general appear to improve, resulting in a sudden widespread surge of progress. Any learning difficulties due to poor concentration would have been 'general' before dominance and 'specific' to an activity or activities after.

A difficult birth could aggravate the need for an initial strategy, or work on the underlying reflexes as in Chapter 11, to bring about an early hemispheric dominance. Identical twins Adam and Bruce, seen in Chapter 3, were coached at home in literacy. Subsequent statementing gave extra support in class continuing into secondary school. In an investigation from January (Year 7) to December (Year 8), the average variability of spellings over successive periods of four sessions was studied. The twin who had a difficult birth appeared to be later in reaching a low figure (Anderson 1997), seemingly because one or more early reflexes were under used and so lingered, hindering the appearance of later reflexes taking their place.

Once established, hemispheric dominance appears to make learning easier by providing a physical basis of concentration. The child then builds his concentration upon this foundation by his own efforts and interests.

# Chapter Seven

## Working On Sidedness For Dominance

We are considering the usual child who has language in the left side of the brain. Just before acquiring dominance, it helps the language side take charge if the other side of the brain is kept as quiet as possible. For that to happen, as many functions as possible should be ordered by the language side of the brain. It means that, ideally, the child should be right-handed, right-footed, right-eyed and right-eared. Thus the relatively quiet, right hemisphere offers less competition to the left side of the brain which is seeking to take charge of language and to be in overall control.

Sometimes, literally by accident, an isolated influence on sidedness has had a logical effect on operating ability. In Year 6, Emma had her left, non-handwriting arm in a plaster for some weeks and when asked if learning seemed easier (a rare leading question) she agreed that it was. When questioned at the end of Year 7, Emma said that it was early in the school year she had become aware of a general easing of her learning difficulties. Conversely, Delacato (1982) tells of a completely right-sided boy whose right arm was put in a cast after an accident. The more he used his left hand the poorer was his reading. When he was able to use his right hand again, his reading improved.

Delacato (1966) states, 'Establishment of hemispheric dominance is the final stage of good neurological development.' He achieves this dominance for his children in a fourth and last step (1982), after exercises for early motor development, by working towards one-sidedness. Delacato used various devices but did not record immobilising the non-dominant arm. The idea of putting a sling on this arm is to prevent neural messages aimed at the dominant hand leaking via the opposite hemispheric motor area to the non-dominant hand; the activation of this area would lead to the general stimulation of that side of the brain which consequently would be better able to attract concentration away from the dominant side.

In January 1971, following a television programme, a Winchester school held a conference where use of the sling was briefly mentioned. A member of staff and one of the audience both said that its benefit came later which was, perhaps, at the acquisition of dominance. The following two examples of a limited number of hour-long periods with the sling on the non-writing arm lend support to the supposition.

## Almost Complete One-Sidedness in Karen

A special reading teacher (SRT) felt she could do nothing more by normal methods for Karen (Year 7) at secondary school and joined in the first of three home visits. Karen thought she wrote mostly with the right (R) hand, and after writing with each in turn, she believed that R was a little easier – it seemed a little faster, too. Other tests of handedness and earedness gave a mixed result. Karen's eyedness was left (L) because an operation had left her R eye weak.

The sleeping-turn was taught in three to ten turns and the evening sleeping work begun (resting 20 minutes in position each morning had not started). Karen's crawling appeared strongly homolateral, but she quickly learnt the sitting-crawl and then managed ten steps crawling on the spot very slowly. She was asked to do two crawls (ten on the spot plus six moving forward) each day for three months. In the walk, her arms and legs were not co-ordinating, the two arms swinging back and forth together sometimes. After teaching the movement, she was asked to do four walks in the house each day for three months.

The next visit was arranged for six weeks later, when Karen's sidedness was still nearly all mixed. However, writing was slightly neater and faster (20 v 24 seconds) with R. Karen's bedtime was 8.30 p.m. and she was not aware of lying awake for long; at 10.30 p.m. mother used to find her in the recovery such position. In crawling there was a slow struggle up to ten 'steps' on the spot; moving forward without breaking rhythm, she was a bit unsteady. Mother thought Karen's walking had to be done slowly, but a slightly faster walk still showed very good co-ordination.

With the writing hand apparently determined, Karen was asked to follow these instructions: (1) Do everything possible with the R hand. (2) Wear a sling for an hour on the L arm each evening while watching television or playing. (3) Play a game each night with the R hand; school kept her supplied with reading games.

Ten weeks later, laterality tests showed vast improvement. Karen was R-handed for throw, comb, toothbrush, eraser and scissors, with L for none; and writing was faster (36 v. 45 seconds) with R – a bigger difference in proportion. The R ear was used at both door and watch on table. The R foot was employed when stamping on a coin at five symmetrical positions just in front, but the foot used when kicking a ball seemed to vary with balance (2R, 2L). It appeared that Karen had done the sling work and game each evening. She usually slept on her side, though was sometimes in position after falling asleep; the morning rest in position which came later would have been appropriate. When crawling, Karen stopped between steps ten and eleven, but explained that she was counting. She reported doing the four walks each evening; good co-ordination was observed even with a faster walk, but Karen's walk tended to be slow.

SRT reported Karen was happier and used phonic analysis to the end of the word, 'holding the length of words', whereas she used to stop in the middle of a long word and guess the remainder. When met nine months later, an experienced special needs teacher who also worked with the girl said that she never ceased 'to be amazed at Karen's improvement'.

Apparently, one-sidedness appeared to be almost completely formed in handedness, earedness and footedness. Also, the increased attention-stretch and widespread improvement suggest it likely that hemispheric dominance had been gained. The dedication to sling work linked with use of reading games suggests what may be the ideal regime. The case study below, demonstrating Simon's use of the sling, provides a more readily attainable target.

## About Fifteen Hours with the Sling

At 10yrs 2m, Simon's handwriting was florid and his early motor movements were checked. Walking was satisfactory, but all crawling steps on the spot were homolateral and his sitting-crawl was weak, though it progressed well in the session. In the sleeping position, his limbs moved independently and twisted awkwardly; they were unwilling to adopt new positions, and were slow and stiff to move.

Handedness was strongly R in writing, erasing, waving and cleaning teeth; whereas eyedness was strongly L in sighting with a rifle, a telescope and a hole in paper pulled to the eyes. Thus, parts of each hemisphere were activated, with a consequent general stimulation of both hemispheres, resulting in their battle for a share of the concentration-flow. A sling on L was recommended for an hour a night to cut down the background activity of the sub-dominant hemisphere.

Revisiting ten weeks later, Simon was found to co-ordinate his crawling and walking well, and to like the sleeping position, which made him feel rested in the morning. Mother estimated that he had worn the sling for about an hour on approximately 15 evenings. After extra phonics twice a week for 15 weeks, he made 11 months and 20 months progress on two word recognition tests, perhaps having gained dominance.

Karen showed how normal school remedial work plus Delacato-type work can transform a child whose learning difficulties at first baffle the special needs teacher. Simon's example suggested that even only 15 sessions of one hour's sling work within a few weeks probably helps to establish a dominant hemisphere.

## Hand in Pocket

A sling may not always be necessary to work on sidedness. A boy (13yrs 7m) whose mother was a head teacher used his right hand for handwriting, catching, and using scissors and eraser; his left hand for tennis, squash, unscrewing a lid and combing; and either hand for brushing his teeth. After testing him and consulting the educational psychologist, the boy was started on the sleeping work (not then including morning rest), the sitting-crawl, crawling 12 steps on the spot and 8 moving forward, and a stilted walk. One night he was found sleeping in position and the next day he received 6½ out of 8 marks in a French spelling test. He had never achieved this level before – 'He would perhaps get half a mark for writing his name,' said his mother. Resourcefully, he had done the test with his left hand in his pocket. (Later he studied Chinese at university.)

The matter is relatively straightforward in the case of right-handers, because immobilising the left hand not only strengthens the handedness, but helps to keep the right hemisphere as inactive as possible while the language hemisphere is developing its dominance.

## The Left-Hander

If the child is left-handed, the relevant motor area is in the right hemisphere, but language, in the usual case, is in the left hemisphere. Before myelination (insulation) of nerve fibres, both hemispheres are active, which must delay the gain of hemispheric dominance. It is no wonder that some teachers of infants have agreed that left-handers are usually later in acquiring basic skills, but catch up eventually.

A second complication may be that the remedial child's left hand is not strongly dominant. Apart from writing with the left hand, he may use it for, say, erasing and waving while throwing and catching with the right hand. Keeping this hand relatively still with a sling for short periods, the path to the left hand can be strengthened.

The teacher in charge of a secondary school remedial department told of a Year 8 boy (reading age 8yrs 5m, spelling age 7yrs 2m) who was left-handed, left-footed and left-eyed. He was extroverted and slow to learn. Reading his book, he followed the words with the left hand while his right hand was tucked in across his lower ribs. The latter hand was making involuntary movements or jerks, so he was asked to sit on it. Immediately, he surprised the two teachers and group of children by reading better and making fewer unexpected errors. The boy even told a student visiting the school that he had to sit on this hand to read properly. So, sitting on the hand provides a third way of immobilising it, at least for short periods.

## Which Hand to Use

When looking for a number in a telephone directory, the index finger of the writing (active) hand is normally used, but when copying the number, it is the non-writing (inactive) hand which points. In general, this hand is used for carrying, holding or resting.

It is important for anyone who thinks that a child's handedness might need to be changed to consult an educational psychologist first. If handedness is partly established, the neural pathways to the hand will have been partly insulated by myelination. So keeping to the preferred hand, before hemispheric dominance, should cause least disturbance to the process. Suzanne Naville, psychomotor therapist in Zurich, said she would only consider changing handedness if there was a tremor as, in her experience, this would be likely to get worse, 'because the child tries to eliminate the tremor by pressing more and more while writing and so he often gets a writer's cramp or he's hurting whenever writing'.

After hemispheric dominance is established with the expected surge of all-round progress, a child may choose to become ambidextrous. Emma, above, changed in the second term at secondary school to writing with her left hand, finding it 'better, neater, faster'. Although unexpected, this was obviously acceptable.

## Sidedness for the Left-Eared Child

One who is left-eared has the main neural connection from the left ear to the right hemisphere. When such a person listens to speech, the message mostly goes from the left ear via the right side of the brain to the left hemisphere. Hence the creative right side inevitably receives general stimulation on the way. Consequently, the language left side is distracted by creative thoughts coming in from the right and, like the left-handed child, one might expect the left-eared child to be late in acquiring dominance.

If the neural pathway from the right ear to the left hemisphere can be improved, it should help to bring an earlier dominance for the language side. This help may be one of the things given when certain workers, after using audiometric tests, stimulate especially the right ear at frequencies in which it is weaker than it should be; an audiometer tests the sensitivity of the ear at different frequencies. Johansen emphasises right ear involvement in his approach. Dr. Berard's sample audiogram (1993, p. 63) shows the left ear weaker at each frequency. Also, Paul Madaule (1994) and Manners emphasise the part to be played by the right ear. Stimulating the right ear is only part of that approach, but if given at a suitable age, it might play an important part in bringing forward a child's dominance.

## Tinted Lenses Might Foster Sidedness

An occupational therapist in Wigan took a child with Irlen spectacles to an optometrist who said that the child became monocular while using them. Where this monocularity happens with children, it would promote sidedness as well as avoiding the problem of poor convergence. The more such children wear the spectacles, the more they might be fostering dominance. (In the next chapter, the state of eyes and ears is considered as a background condition affecting the degree of switching off.)

At about the time that the language hemisphere gains dominance, it is said that approximately 30% to 50% of the brain's neural pathways die off, which seems to be a necessary consequence. One might expect that the extent of destruction would depend on the strength of dominance acquired, and perhaps this reduction would not take place at all if dominance remains shared by the hemispheres.

# Chapter Eight

## Primary And Secondary Factors

### Factors Favouring Maintenance of Attention

It was puzzling that the four children from a class of top infants who could not do a brisk cross-pattern walk satisfactorily were among the best readers. It seems that other favourable, more powerful factors probably influenced them, making it unnecessary to consider their poor marching.

A child whose verbal ability, motivation and emotional stability are strong is likely to maintain the focus of his attention in spite of inadequate rest, unsatisfactory cross-pattern movement, mixed sidedness and poor conditions of work. That is, if the primary factors are strong, it does not matter if the secondary factors are weak. A comparison might be made with sunlight and moonlight: if the sun is shining, it does not matter how much the moon is, or is not, shining.

Moonlight is not valued until the sun has gone down. Similarly, if a child has learning difficulties and his 'sunshine factors' are weak, his moonlight factors become important. Aiding the secondary factors of adequate rest, satisfactory cross-pattern rhythm, one-sidedness and suitable conditions allows learning to proceed slowly but surely.

### Concentration – a Different Dimension

With regard to dyslexic children, Pumphrey and Reason (1991) were not happy with single-factor theories, but the idea put here is a two-factor theory: we have teachable learning difficulties plus poor concentration due to an excessive number of tiny switch-offs. These are problems in different dimensions and the second can be alleviated on its own with notable results. This factor of poor concentration is itself caused by many factors.

If thought of as a flow, concentration involves transmission from one hemisphere to the other, i.e. 'horizontal' movement. Most educational studies deal with interaction between the relating hemisphere and something which might be related, i.e. 'vertical' interaction. Usually investigations report what the child can do when he is presumed to be switched in; whereas the present study is about trying to keep it that way, by minimising the switch-offs which cause disruption.

Thus, any difficulty in learning could be resolved into horizontal and vertical components. The child may have lost the 'vertical' application to the task because he has largely switched off 'horizontally' to the other side of the brain. In spelling, for example, if the average variability remains over, say, 33%, one can attend to the horizontal component of concentration. The normal study of spelling is the vertical component.

In handwriting, each time a child switches off he may alter the slope and size of his letters, with many switch-offs bringing many variations. Letter formation may alter: a switch-off while writing 'baby' might result in forming each 'b' in a different way; and there may be a constant changing between alternative forms of 's'.

Learning to read the basic key words might be hindered by the vertical component of poor visual discrimination, but if the child shows extreme variability during matching exercises, the horizontal component of concentration warrants assistance. Later in reading, there may be a problem in his knowing where to pause between phrases, made worse by his switching off at inopportune moments.

## The Horizontal Component of Concentration

The horizontal component of concentration is particularly important before the child's dominance is formed and while his switching off is excessive. Switching off is one causal factor of learning difficulties, but has, itself, many causal factors, as can be seen in Figure 16.

Inadequacies in:

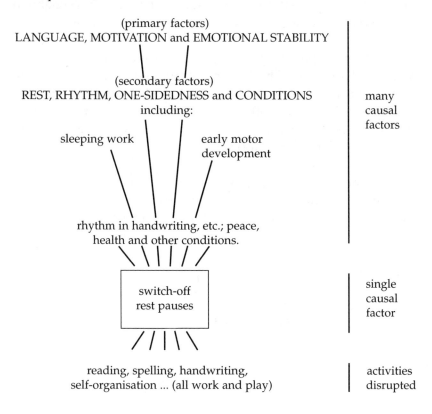

(primary factors)
LANGUAGE, MOTIVATION and EMOTIONAL STABILITY

(secondary factors)
REST, RHYTHM, ONE-SIDEDNESS and CONDITIONS
including:

sleeping work        early motor
                     development

rhythm in handwriting, etc.; peace,
health and other conditions.

switch-off
rest pauses

reading, spelling, handwriting,
self-organisation ... (all work and play)

many
causal
factors

single
causal
factor

activities
disrupted

**Figure 16** *Many Factors but One Factor*

Any or all of many factors cause the single factor of switch-off rest pauses: this single factor in turn may disrupt one or more activities. If the primary factors are strong, the secondary factors are not so important. However, if the main factors are weak, the child is more dependent on the minor factors. When positive, these include adequate rest, rhythm (of which cross-pattern movement seems an important one), sidedness (implying minimum activity of the sub-dominant side of the brain), and agreeable working conditions. Also, instances affecting the degree of switching off have seemed to include illness, recent exertion, a busy environment, the prospect of returning to a disturbed home atmosphere, the visit of a separated parent, and even beloved grandparents leaving on holiday.

The 'quick and careless' approach (see 'fast-inaccurate readers' in Appendix 3) of some children must aggravate the problem of switching off. An inappropriately quickened rhythm may readily overload the brain and allow a switch-off in the middle of a task-chunk, causing errors as seen in Chapter 6. Obviously, suiting the rhythm to the task is important.

The excitement at Christmas has its down side, too. During the year's study of switch-off errors in reading at the Remedial Reading Centre, from the first week of December, those errors of nearly all juniors began to increase: not until the week before the Christmas holidays did this increase happen with the secondary school children.

## Other Conditions May Disturb Concentration

Other major areas of concern may affect a child's concentration. Poor vision, hearing, nutrition and health will, at least, create disturbing conditions, making it difficult for him to keep his attention on the task; the discomfort distracts the child and aggravates switching off. So, this distraction due to discomfort is one more reason to carry out normal testing of the child's eyes and ears.

Helen Irlen (1991) tests children to find out if tinted lenses aid vision by removing distortions of text when reading. Comparable results are found using an Intuitive Colorimeter, available at certain optometric practices, a list of which may be obtained from the Institute of Optometry in London (also see Harris & MacRow-Hill 1998).

## Keep Working on the Primary Factors

When hemispheric dominance is achieved, much of the involuntary nature of switching off will be removed. However, the habit often remains, so it is particularly important to maintain the powerful influence of the primary factors. For example, it has been said that we can often talk our way out of problems, but the child doing so needs motivation and emotional stability. Fortunately, becoming motivated in even one subject often seems to galvanise a listless child. Thus, while attending to the above secondary factors with a child, we have to develop the primary factors as much as possible.

# Chapter Nine

## Variable Spelling; Dominance And Dyslexia

Spelling variability is a useful aid in monitoring the rate of switching off in spelling. A 26-year-old labourer wished to take 'O' Level examinations, but, troubled with spelling all his life, he wanted to know if he was dyslexic. If his development was late, two factors might have promoted it: his left-sidedness (strong in hand, foot and eye) and the breaking of his eventual writing arm at three years of age. However, he brought a letter, of about 120 words, in neat writing, which often appears to accompany the apparent gain of dominance. The four words spelt incorrectly, including 'possible/possable', were given as a spelling test. Three were the same in the test as in the letter, and one was different: 25% 'variability' of spellings on this small sample.

If this score was typical of him, he had probably achieved his hemispheric dominance, yet he needed to remove the wrong spellings gathered when switching off a lot. Not a beginning speller, he was asked to look up difficult words in the dictionary, add them to a list underlining the tricky parts, and look through such lists from time to time.

Of course, even a speller considered satisfactory must be allowed some variability, because he may occasionally wish to select a different spelling when rewriting a word he is unsure of. Allowing this minimum, the average variability of spelling in a special double dictation, such as that shown in Appendix 5, should give a better impression of average ability to keep switched in, at least to dictation. A child recording high variability under these conditions might be physically unable to maintain attention well in other subjects requiring a similar integration of complex sensory information.

A primitive report of evening research on hemispheric 'dominance and the variability of spellings' was distributed to some experts in specific learning difficulties/dyslexia, in May 1975. The next year, another expert, a friend of one of those receiving a copy, spoke to an invited audience at Preston. A senior college lecturer and an educational psychologist each reported him as saying, 'Dyslexic children do variable spellings. Non-dyslexic children do not do variable spellings.'

In this case, he was reported to have tested variability of spellings with the same dictation an hour later. In my earlier research reported to him, parents repeated a dictation from the child's reading book 24 hours later. Dictations stopped at a natural place after 10 to 15 errors had been made. Years later, the speaker could not remember his reported claim, but a more accurate statement can be suggested now and is offered below.

## Dyslexia – Delayed Dominance Plus Learning Difficulties?

Specific learning difficulties (SpLD) and dyslexia are considered to be approximately interchangeable terms at present. However, dyslexia implies a cause whereas SpLD does not. Should a cause be found, the situation would change; educators would be able to work at removing the cause of the problem. If SpLD/dyslexia might be equated with many switch-off rest pauses at an unexpectedly late age plus teachable learning difficulties, it could be expressed as follows: dyslexia equals delayed dominance plus standard learning difficulties. Variability of performance becomes important and, in particular, the measurement of spelling variability usually makes some sense when averaged over a few sessions.

Relating variability of spelling to dyslexia brings into question the age at which a child might be considered dyslexic. Young infants show variability but are not so labelled: for example, most five-year-olds will have much variability of performance, indicating incomplete hemispheric dominance. On the other hand, a ten-year-old with such characteristics is considered a problem. The generalisation that 'Dyslexic children do variable spellings' will not do for both.

The expert's reported statement might be restated: 'Children without spelling dominance do many variable spellings: children who have this dominance do few, if any, variable spellings.' It appears self-evident if one accepts dominance as being accompanied by the reduction of switch-offs from excessive to sparse. The consequence of switching off is particularly obvious in special double dictations in which the second dictation specifically requires recall of the first.

In one article on dyslexia, it was stated that most children seem to emerge from their learning problems by 11 years of age. Perhaps this emergence is because so many of the children respond to the new interests fostered at their secondary school. The new-found motivation may provide the final impetus to establish a dominant language side of the brain.

There can be little doubt that most children gain their dominance while in junior school. Children who are needlessly late in acquiring their hemispheric dominance, or 'boss side of the brain', should be a cause of concern. Their education must suffer in proportion to the lateness. Certainly, we do not want them to enter secondary school with as much as 100% variability of spelling, suggesting dominance is far from established.

With regard to a threshold, children with a spelling variability over 33% readily accept the work on a physical basis of concentration, and when it is lowered even a little to 20% to 25% they often feel ready to finish. A good example of this was provided by one restless, disadvantaged Year 5 boy (co-operative in a one-to-one situation) whose concentration was helped at school only for non-confrontational behaviour problems. He asked in a typically forthright manner, 'Can I finish?', which the leader was actually considering for him: that session's 'variability' brought his average for three consecutive sessions down to 24%.

When a child 'finishes', he is asked to keep up a maintenance programme of sleeping work, walking and crawling until he is aware of a widespread surge of progress which almost certainly denotes the acquisition of a general dominance, and until his learning difficulties no longer seem a problem to him.

# Chapter Ten

## Reducing Variability

### Use of Sleeping Work and Exercises

By the time of variability testing, some children were helped with spelling only, some with spelling variability only, and others with both. Susan and Joseph were taught spelling as a pair throughout Years 4, 5 and 6 and were willing to continue below 20% in variability work.

In Year 5, Susan's average spelling variability decreased over a few months of weekly double mini-dictations: 56%, 31%, 23%. She had done the sleeping work, sitting-crawl and frog wriggle, which were monitored in the occasional home visit. However, by July Susan wanted to give up the exercises and, without saying so, she gave up the sleeping routine too. From September to February of Year 6, her average variability was back to 31%.

Then two things happened which revitalised the programme. Susan's mother suggested checking the exercises at school, which became the norm: exercises set were monitored once a week with the children in pairs. At the same time, Karen's record summarised in Chapter 7 was re-read, so the children's sidedness was tested. Where this was mixed, a little sling work was added to the exercises given, after which sidedness was normally tested again to see if it was better established.

Susan's sidedness was found satisfactory: her sleeping work was resumed, and her crawling and walking were checked. Crawling forward showed confusion with signs of homolateral movement remaining even four weeks later: thereafter, her crawling was very good. In the two periods of four weeks each from February, her average variabilities were 16% and 5%. During the last few weeks before the summer holiday, the variability of most children tended to rise erratically: perhaps longer daylight and physically tiring

69

activities increased switching off. Probably due to this tendency to rise, Susan averaged 26% over the last five weeks. Incidentally, she was easily the fastest sprinter on sports day (see 'Sporting benefits', Chapter 12).

## The Addition of Sling Work

Joseph was reserved and often seemed tired. In Year 5, he produced average variabilities of 52%, 30%, 33%, 52% and began the next year scoring averages of 39%, 39%. His exercises were fair, but he would not rest in the sleeping position. After discussion with his parents, Joseph put a sling on the non-writing arm ten minutes an evening for five weeks. Becoming much keener, he reported doing it every day and also lying in position for 20 minutes most mornings: spelling variability in that period was little different at 35%. In the half-term before the summer holiday, possibly having sensed the value of the sling work, Joseph was willing to do it for six weeks, aiming at a minimum 15 sessions of one hour, which followed Simon in Chapter 7. Each week he claimed three sessions, notching up 18. In the first three weeks Joseph's average was down to 14%, though in the last three weeks of the summer term, with two very late nights, his average was high. The scattered signs of left-sidedness in hands, eyes and ears remained after the two periods of sling work, but footedness became slightly more right-sided. He retained an interest in the work, perhaps appreciating its value to him.

Right-handed Mark (Year 6) was probably an underachieving, bright boy performing at an average level. While there were no complaints about his classwork, he showed up in the September class check, and scored 100% variability on each of his first two weekly double dictations. Mark and his parents had been conscious of something wrong with his concentration. Before the exercises began, his average variability was 65%; after they commenced it was 62%. Later, while Mark had a sling on the non-writing arm for 10 to 15 minutes on 29 out of 35 evenings, his variability was down to 50%. During the last six weeks of the summer term, Mark was willing to use the sling for an hour per evening trying to achieve 15 sessions; he reported weeks of 6, 2, 3, 3, 3, 0 sessions; variability was down to 33%.

With hands, feet, eyes and ears, Mark gave five indications of left-sidedness at first (three out of three catches with the left hand was one, and another was left foot stamping on the middle coin of five spread laterally in front of him); there was only one indication after the sling work.

Work on reflexes was suggested as it might relate to the remaining high variability – high considering the assistance given. Another incident seemed to add weight to the recommendation: it appeared odd that when photographs were being taken he was continually stopped from leaning over to his right. Jane Field (1992) states that 'if you have an aberrant Tonic Labyrinthine Reflex (TLR) then your Head Righting Reflexes will be inefficient'. The TLR is a reflex which should be present at birth to affect the child's balance if, in a prone or supine position, his head is lifted above or lowered below the level of the spine; but the TLR must then be inhibited to allow the permanent Head Righting Reflexes to develop completely. Gwen Wilkinson (1994) after research on a small group suggests 'that the TLR may underlie the cluster of reflexes which appear to contribute to underachievement and learning difficulty in the normal classroom'. Subsequently, Mark was taken for some work on his aberrant reflexes, but did not complete the course.

There was quite a different outcome for another Year 6 boy who showed 100% 'variability' in his first session: he followed this score with 20%, 33%, 0%, 0%, leaving him with a satisfactory average.

The value of one-sidedness might be adversely affected by emotional upset. One example was a disturbed child, about seven years old, who attended an appropriate unit daily, but was seen privately at his temporary home. His sleeping routine, walking and crawling were progressing. He was strongly right-sided in hand, eye, ear and foot, yet his learning difficulties remained great. Probably, the primary factor of emotional problems kept switching him off, in spite of aid from the secondary factor of one-sidedness. As he was about to return to his difficult home situation, his bed-wetting returned and he could cope no longer with the sleeping work.

Left-handed Colin (Year 5) recorded average variabilities of 67% before exercises began, 35% as exercises were gradually introduced, and 28% while the sling was used on the non-writing arm for five weeks at 10 minutes an evening, using it a reported five to seven times a week. Sidedness checked before and after the 10 minutes, sling work was not much affected. After the summer holiday and during a half-term of 31% average variability, Colin lost interest in this work, perhaps due to satisfaction with his reduced variability or to the influence of home or both. His parents were not equally strict.

## Temporary Dominance

Judging by improved variability in spelling or reading, or by better general concentration, a child may appear to have dominance when doing exercises; however, he may lose it as variability worsens when he stops them. It was pointed out that Susan reverted to higher variability of spelling when the sleeping routine, sitting-crawl and frog wriggle were given up. After the sleeping work was restarted with crawling added, her variability fell again.

When help was primarily with reading, reversals seemed affected in a similar way to variability of spelling later. A private junior pupil helped with reading did only one reversal in the 12th session; so the sleeping work, crawling and walking were stopped. When seen next, he was 'full of reversals' again as his mother had said, so the programme was resumed. We saw his reversals clear up straightaway.

Holly, in Year 9, showed poor concentration and did bizarre spellings. She was helped one-to-one by an SpLD support teacher. Holly began following fairly closely stage 1 of Delacato's 'New Start' (1982):

1. Sleeping work: Mother checked her position on going to bed and later once when she was asleep.
2. One-sided (homolateral) wriggling: This was done on a groundsheet for a smooth surface; by alternating the sleeping positions she produced a forward sliding movement.

3.  Hearing: The right ear was covered with the right hand for four one-minute periods of conversation daily; this procedure was repeated with left hand over left ear.
4.  Visual practice: One eye followed an object held in her hand on the same side of her body.

Her concentration became better and spellings improved from bizarre to phonetic. However, when Holly began stage 2 she felt unable to do the crawling because the bedroom was not big enough; concentration and spellings deteriorated.

It was suggested that Holly was given the sleeping work plus the sitting-crawl and no ear or eye exercises. Spelling errors again became phonetic and better concentration returned. Father reported co-ordination was better and Holly claimed to be able to see where to play a pass in hockey.

Incidentally, Holly wore Helen Irlen tinted spectacles, which she was sure helped her. If these restricted her to using one eye, a possibility which has been suggested, they could have reduced conflict between opposing hemispheres.

# Chapter Eleven

## The Underlying Reflexes – A Safety Net

Should any of the early motor movements be difficult while variability remains high, one can develop the underlying reflexes. Included in these difficulties should be the inability to sleep all night in position. Though this difficulty includes rather a lot of us, it is particularly those upper junior and lower secondary school children who demonstrate a high variability of performance, such as, say, over 33% spelling variability, whom we are most concerned about here. It suggests that hemispheric dominance has not been established, and it needs to be, the sooner the better.

A considerable number of reflexes seem to be involved in normal movement (Jean Pyfer 1988). Barbara Rider (1972) found that children with learning difficulties, but without 'any observable physical disability or excessive inco-ordination ... demonstrated significantly more abnormal reflex responses than the normal second-grade children.' Also, those children in the control group without abnormal reflex responses were superior on standard tests in reading, spelling and arithmetic to the controls showing abnormal responses. These comments emphasise the importance of reflexes in basic education. Jane Field (1995) briefly describes some reflexes assessed in neuro-developmental work. She adds, 'Work on suppressing primitive, or immature, reflexes frees the cortex from conscious control of movement. This allows for more concentration to be devoted to learning.' Sally Goddard (1996) expands on this theme.

### The Institute for Neuro-Physiological Psychology

Dr. Peter Blythe of the Institute for Neuro-Physiological Psychology (INPP) corrects aberrant reflexes in children with SpLD (specific learning difficulties), emphasising that 'it is a very small and concise thing'. Associates and others, trained in this approach, are available in different parts of the country to treat such conditions.

At the Institute, the earlier testing of early motor movements as described by Delacato was replaced by checking for the aberrant presence of the primitive reflexes so therapists 'could examine the Central Nervous System for dysfunction with accuracy' (Blythe 1990). Field and Blythe (1995) and Goddard (1996) give tests for finding a number of aberrant reflexes. These are inhibited with 'a personalised Reflex-Inhibition programme each day at home' taking 'approximately 4 to 14 minutes' (Blythe 1992). He refers to exercises as 'management patterns' (WLAP tape).

In the rare cases where primitive reflexes are missing, some experts even introduce the reflexes before eliminating them. Jane Field adds, 'Sometimes Primitive Reflexes have not become properly established. If this is so, they must be brought to their full expression before they can be inhibited or transformed; the way is then clear for the Postural Reflexes to become efficient.'

## The Tonic Neck Reflex

An example of what should happen is when a baby, born in the normal way, uses the asymmetric tonic neck reflex (atnr) to assist it into the world; on turning the head to one side the baby takes the 'fencer' position and the limb movements assist expulsion (Goddard 1991). 'This should be present at birth and inhibited while awake by 6 months of life,' she writes (1990). Later, the symmetric tonic neck reflex (stnr) must be inhibited before the child can control and hold his head when crawling: appearing 'at between 6 to 8 months... (the stnr) should be inhibited by about 11 months' (Field 1992). The importance of this reflex in the work of O'Dell and Cook is mentioned in Chapter 2. The transformed tonic neck reflex (ttnr) is the recommended sleeping position shown in Figures 7 & 12.

The frog wriggle might moderate the severity of an aberrant stnr (i.e. an stnr retained too long). Twins Adam and Bruce, at ten years of age, mastered the progression within two weeks. Both appeared to spend all night in the sleeping position once during the second week; their father checked them first thing in the morning before leaving for work. By five weeks, the older twin appeared to sleep in position all the time. He was asked to stop the frog wriggle and the family were to observe changes in the sleeping; the other twin wished to follow suit. The next week, each boy appeared to spend only three nights in position.

Perhaps the stnr (possibly influenced by the frog wriggle) was not fully inhibited, and so the ttnr was unable to act powerfully the whole night. Nevertheless, the twins were reported to show widespread improvement in classwork; while the younger, who had been in danger of 'giving up' at school, gained a renewed interest. Both soon received a statement from an educational psychologist which brought help from an SpLD support teacher.

Work on the reflexes underlying the early motor movements may be used as a 'safety net' if the Delacato-type exercises remain difficult. However, even resorting to reflexes, the sleeping routine should still be followed, for it is basic and affects a child's work and play so much.

## Tracing Weaknesses Directly to Reflexes

Some educational weaknesses can be traced directly to inadequate reflex development. For example, Jane Field (1989, 1990) explains how postural difficulties in handwriting are traced to uninhibited asymmetric and symmetric tonic neck reflexes (i.e. two reflexes which should have been inhibited earlier and which are interfering with intended movements). It appears second best and a labour of love for a teacher to repeat endlessly, 'Stretch up (head and upper body) to save your eyes'; though the effect lasts longer than with, 'Keep your head up'. Sally Goddard Blythe and David Hyland (1998) include tracing many weaknesses to retained primitive reflexes.

The transformed tonic neck reflex usually appears by about eight months (Blythe 1990), and does not come to its fullest expression until the earlier forms of the tonic neck reflex have been inhibited, so a baby should not be put in this position early, which suggestion fits in with the current practice of putting babies on their backs. As mentioned, to sleep in position, the child should have the reflexes enabling him to turn completely onto his back if too hot.

If a child is still frustrated by learning difficulties after improved early motor development, he can be checked on a wide range of reflexes by a specialist. Persons aged from 2½ all the way to 73 years have had their reflexes trained.

Aberrant reflex profiles are those which show that some reflexes which should have been inhibited have not been inhibited and are affecting movement; consequently, reflexes which normally appear in their place have not been able to establish themselves well. If we can consider that such aberrant reflex profiles and early motor development problems are related, they might be divided into three stages of severity:

1. When the child's reflex profile is too immature, treatment of the reflex problems is probably required early to avoid stress during later movement training.

2. If the problem is a little less severe, there may be prolonged difficulty with exercises closely related to early motor development, so that work on the underlying reflexes would be adviable.

3. With a greater number of children who have only mild reflex and early motor development problems, an initial strategy based on the Delacato idea should be enough to ensure an early hemispheric dominance. Even before that is attained, general performance is likely to improve because the tests on Rider's control group (see earlier comment) suggest that reflexes are relevant to the children's attainment.

# Chapter Twelve

## Implications And Applications

The first two types of child, below, are the main ones who have been assisted by work based on the proposed theory. The idea supports accepted present practice in education such as multisensory teaching for SpLD/Dyslexia, a period of effort with neat cursive writing, and simultaneous reading. Also, there are links with many areas such as autism and epilepsy, and there are various unclassified instances; all of which, to different extents, tend to confirm the widespread usefulness of the theory. Behaviour difficulties are discussed in Appendix 4.

### The Mainstream Child in Years 2 to 4 Who Cannot Blend

In children of Years 2 to 4 who could not blend words such as 'cat, dog', perfecting the sitting-crawl almost invariably allowed the child to blend them. One might postulate that the improved cross-pattern movement stabilises the brain-stem partially, increasing the attention-stretch enough for the child to blend phonically regular three-letter words between tiny switch-offs.

### The Older Mainstream Child, Usually in Years 5 to 8, with High Spelling Variability

A child's spelling seems usually susceptible to his poor general concentration. In many cases, if children with an average spelling variability of over 33% have it reduced to the region of 20% to 25%, they are much less frustrated by inadequate concentration. To work on sleeping, crawling and walking where there are weaknesses may be enough, but the initial strategy should extend to work on other early motor development, if necessary. Should concentration difficulties still remain, sidedness may be improved with the sling work strengthening neural pathways to the writing hand. With a small number of children, specialist help for the underlying reflexes might be needed to help with difficult early motor movements.

Also, a child may prefer to fall asleep in position although staying asleep in it for only five minutes, and may practice lying for 20 minutes awake in position the next morning; but, if he wishes to sleep in the recovery position all night, specialist help with reflexes is likely to be needed. However, the immediate objective of the initial strategy is both to remove frustration caused by poor concentration and to bring forward hemispheric dominance as seen in a wide-ranging surge of learning ability. An early dominance may also be encouraged by specialist help for eyes and ears, in addition to any other benefit so obtained.

## Wider Implications

*Early mobility on the floor*
Babies should have as much time as possible on the floor for strong early motor development. Baby bouncers and walkers do not allow the natural development of reflexes.

*Early schooling*
In toddler groups, playgroups and nursery schools, an attempt might be made to check and assist where necessary as much early motor development as possible. Parents might be encouraged to put their child in the sleeping position once each night, providing that the child can be relied upon to turn onto his back if too hot; it is not good enough for the child to turn his head and not the remainder of his body in the same direction. **A baby should definitely not be put on its front in the recovery position.**

*The non-writing hand in reading*
In the earliest stages, the beginning reader should use the writing hand when pointing (with the index finger) or holding a card under a line. If the non-writing hand keeps moving, he can sit on it with a view to firming up his handedness.

*Simultaneous reading*
In simultaneous reading, the child learns to read in phrases which, apart from organising meaning, helps to channel switch-offs into natural breaks. It is worth doing until a child is able to phrase and keeps doing so.

*A period of very neat cursive writing*
A child, usually a junior, should be encouraged to do very neat cursive writing for a period, until there is a surge of progress. Particular care with writing is often taken about the time that dominance is gained. Perhaps this taking care occurs naturally because switch-offs are more likely to fall in the gaps between words when the pen or pencil is lifted from the paper. This incidence should cause less interruption to the writing and to the development of dominance, after which the child simply writes to suit the needs of the occasion.

*Multisensory teaching for SpLD/Dyslexia*
Hulme and Bradley (1984) found that the visual-auditory-motor (VAM) teaching of spelling they tested was much more effective for the retarded readers than their VM and VA methods. Professor Tim Miles (1990) asserts that any theory of dyslexia must show why multisensory teaching is so successful.

From the present viewpoint, a child might switch off in one or more sensory channels, yet not in every channel employed. He might avoid a complete switch-off in a task by keeping attention on it through one or more channels, so allowing concentration in the switch-off channel or channels to rejoin after a rest pause. The effect is to reduce too many switch-offs to a manageable number, causing less disruption.

*Good speller underachieving*
A good speller with 100% variability may be accepted as an average pupil, yet be very dissatisfied with his level of achievement. His effective ability satisfying the needs of the teacher may hide the child's poor concentration, because passable spelling might mask its high fluctuation. The variability of spelling may be checked if a parent feels their child in an upper junior class or lower secondary school class is not rated high enough. The initial strategy described here should immediately ease the problem before work on the underlying reflexes is considered.

*Phrased and unhurried delivery*
Some teachers and parents speak to their children too quickly. It is better that delivery of speech should be phrased and unhurried, giving the children time to attend to and process the message. Also, the teacher or parent should not begin until all children have had a moment to build up the maximum attention for listening; important information should not be given in the first phrases but should follow a preamble. Such care is especially important for children whose difficulties include poor concentration.

*Autism*
It is possible that either the build-up of concentration-flow is shared equally between the sides of the brain or the main centre of concentration see-saws between the two hemispheres. The result is that when the language side tries to make an utterance, the other side interrupts with a confusing and equally strong message, so no speech comes out.

A child without dominance might sing an alphabet song, or the autistic youth play the harpsichord, once shown on television. The brain achieves a temporary control by the 'music' hemisphere due to tonal stimulation. When the music stops, the equality of dominance re-asserts itself.

Some progress can be attempted, using a temporary dominance on the non-language side, by teaching through the medium of music. This possibility fits in with Bakker's idea (1990, *et al.* 1995) that, for the normal child, reading benefits initially from using right hemisphere strategies before moving over to left hemisphere use.

On the other hand, the sleeping work and early motor development approach to maintaining attention offers ways of developing dominance on the language side. An Autistic Centre in the London area was reported to achieve some success using the ideas of Delacato, whose book on autism (1974) is still obtainable. Also, Stella Carlton (1993) writing in *The Other Side of Autism* considers that the development of certain reflexes may be relevant.

*Epilepsy*
In epilepsy, switch-offs are likely to be more severe than those considered up to now. The main build-up of concentration would

probably not only flow over to the pictures side but also down into the brain-stem (see Figure 1). The typical weakness of epileptic children in mathematics, reported by one of their headteachers, fits in with the idea that the concentration-flow at a switch-off cannot be held on the pictures side of the brain where some mathematics is thought to be done, but carries on down into the brain-stem. Work on the physical basis of concentration may therefore have some relevance.

*Schizophrenia*
It is said that 'we are two people', of which a Jekyll and Hyde personality is an extreme example. Schizophrenia literally means splitting in the mind; it could be due to a conflict between the two hemispheres of the brain. The language and naturally relating side would tend to have warm thoughts towards others, whereas the poorer, relating and more self-aware side would be comparatively cooler to others (see below). If the bulk of concentration see-saws between the hemispheres, the subject's personality might seem to alternate. In extreme cases the person could appear to be good one moment and bad the next, when he switched over to be controlled by the other side of the brain. Weaknesses, like those referred to in this book, might aggravate the condition, in which case it would be useful to work on them establishing a missing hemispheric dominance, perhaps in social relationships.

*Chronic fatigue syndrome CFS/ME*
The existence of this disability is not completely and universally recognised. However, one might suppose that if sleeping in the recovery position promotes rest much more than does lying on the back, as the investigation in Chapter 3 suggests, then some people may never be thoroughly rested. Some sufferers may not have discovered the most restful sleeping position available to them, and this may constitute part of their problem.

*Mental and physical disability*
Inadequate concentration is likely to be one of the problems of the child with a mental and physical disability, where their normal development has been disturbed. David McGlown, Director of The Centre for Brain Injury Rehabilitation and Development (BIRD), Chester, devotes a chapter to 'The Importance of Reflexes in Development' in *Developmental Reflexive Rehabilitation* (1990).

*Possible link with cot-deaths*

Cot-deaths occur mostly in the first ten months of an infant's life. The transformed tonic neck reflex (ttnr) usually emerges at eight months and, while the child sleeps on his front, it tends to put him in the recovery position. However, if the asymmetric tonic neck reflex and symmetric tonic neck reflex have not been inhibited to make way for the emergence of the ttnr, there could be confused movement when the child is in the sleeping position. For example, a baby in the recovery position might turn his head while the remainder of his body does not move, because the reflex linking them – the transformed tonic neck reflex – is not in place until eight months and perhaps later. This turn of the head would cause tension around the neck. (See 'Early schooling' above.)

*Stress at the workplace*

Stress at the workplace is often a concern, and can be a problem aggravated by lack of rest. An example is the tired shop assistant who is easily distracted from serving and has an almost stationary queue. Twenty minutes of rest in the recovery position before rising should help her to be more fit for work.

*A cause of accidents*

An aircraft approaching an airport in former Yugoslavia was being talked down in the dark: the pilot turned left instead of right and hit a mountain. Train drivers, signal installers and software programmers are among those who could suffer similarly from a bad switch-off at the wrong moment. A tapping test, as seen in Appendix 2, might serve to check whether applicants for certain jobs occasionally suffer longish switch-offs. Some work on aberrant reflexes or even the initial strategy might conceivably help. Again the sleeping work seems basic.

*More problems with boys, initially*

A greater number of boys than girls have SpLD. Girls generally enjoy using language more than boys, resulting in extra practice, so that on average the girls probably gain their dominant language side earlier. Boys' learning difficulties are likely to appear greater because, dominance being late, their excessive switching off lasts longer.

In other problem areas, too, there are three or four times more boys than girls, and this makes a late hemispheric dominance seem a possible common causal factor. However, the difference in numbers between the sexes doesn't necessarily hold among those students needing dyslexia support at university. This lack of difference was the case at York and should be expected when boys have caught up with girls in gaining their dominance.

Until then, boys will appear to lag behind girls in some respects. It would explain why, socially, girls in the early teens are more advanced, and why girls normally appear to achieve better at school. There is a clear need for all children to achieve hemispheric dominance as soon as possible, allowing them to benefit more from their education.

### Sporting benefits

Svea Gold says, and reports Delacato and Blythe as agreeing, that this kind of work can be recommended to children for the sporting benefits it produces which are usually more important to them than help with learning difficulties. Here is an example of this bonus.

The two elder brothers of Clive in Chapter 3 were given the sleeping work and walking because they wanted it, the difference in their age range being about three years. On the second home visit two weeks later, the eldest, Alan, knew the sleeping position on the floor and did a steady turn; walking was 'smooth, co-ordinated and good'. Brian, the middle boy, received assistance with the sleeping position, having a strong tendency to both bend the wrong leg and do a jerky turn; he walked with feet in line, tending to lose balance until corrected. Alan reported that having begun this work he could beat Brian at running which previously he could not do.

### School dinners

It might be self-evident that a child with concentration problems should be encouraged to have school dinners rather than 'sandwiches' (assuming his diet is supervised), for they provide sustained, balanced nutrition hard to match when pressures at home begin to take effect on snack preparation.

At the very least, the protracted loss of an essential nutrient must disadvantage the brain and stimulate extra switching off: the hyperactive child's need for zinc is well known, and Vitamin B6 supplements have been found particularly useful in treating hyperactivity and autism (Foresight 1998).

*Feeling warm or cool towards others*
When a person walks into a room, we often warm to them: our concentration is switched to the language side of the brain as we give them attention. As they leave, we withdraw attention and sometimes feel a little less warm towards them; the concentration which was given them might flow from the language side of the brain to the poorer-relating and more self-interested side of the brain. So the words side tends to be associated with warm, outgoing, generous feelings, whereas the creative side tends to produce cool, self-concerned, less generous thoughts.

*Some old people switch off more*
It is likely that at least some old people tend to switch off more. An 82-year-old wrote: 'Mary wa (was) not s (so) lucky.' She added that she could hardly spell for her memory 'fades away'. Some old people seem to predominantly use the creative/poorly responding side of the brain, perhaps because they find it difficult to hold their concentration on the better-relating side. In effect, they are in a second infanthood – the 'second childhood'. An interest in art, craft and music keeps giving pleasure to what is at least for them the lower side of the brain, when rising to the verbal side for prolonged periods becomes impossible.

It seems relevant to suggest that some world-class batsmen and snooker players, for example, appear to continue playing well when past their prime, but lose their mastery through making more slips. To maintain concentration on the task becomes just that bit harder with age as almost imperceptible switch-offs have greater effect.

*Children crossing the road*
If children were taught to 'look both ways twice' when crossing the road, repetition of the task would allow time for the build-up of concentration on the relating side of the brain. Thus, greater attention could be directed to possible dangers.

## Unclassified Instances

The theory also appears to be relevant in the following unclassified instances:

*Co-ordination of eyes*
One of Lucy's eyes kept wandering to the side and the previous teacher at the Reading Centre considered her 'blind' in the right eye. Early motor movements were checked: the hands did 'various orbits' in the bicycling exercise; the hand tended to rise and fall before the knee in the then-used homolateral crawl. Later, after help and when Lucy was in Year 8, her eyes seemed to co-ordinate well, which mother did not disagree with, although observing that her eye was still weak.

Recently, Svea Gold wrote of a boy with crossed eyes who was prescribed +5 lenses by the optometrist to straighten them out, but, fortunately, the family did nothing about the glasses and his other ones broke. Part of his work, during half-hour sessions, five days a week, was symmetrical tonic reflex inhibition and (English) crawling. The symmetrical tonic neck reflex has to be inhibited before the child can progress from a crawling stance. After six weeks, because he would have to have glasses for the start of school, he was sent back to the optometrist, who 'now wanted to put only +1 lenses on him, and those only for reading.'

*Crawling upstairs to bed*
Natalie (7yrs 8m) was said to have a poor memory which 'ran' in the family, and she crawled upstairs to bed. She made a fair start to the sitting-crawl and reported the sleeping position to be 'nice and comfy'. Four days later, she said that she had fallen asleep in position on two nights; the sitting-crawl was almost perfect. On the fifth day: 'The crawl is making my legs better – working together better,' but she still had to crawl upstairs to bed. On the eleventh day: 'Don't have to crawl upstairs on my hands and knees any more.'

*Aid in falling asleep*
One child reported surprise at going to sleep very quickly after doing the sitting-crawl at bedtime, an experience which two others in the group later claimed to verify. 'Oh yes, it's true,' said

one, sure of himself. (A girl in the group who had not been given the sitting-crawl fancied trying it at bedtime, but said there was no difference.) Years later, Emma in Year 6 (seen twice in Chapter 7), volunteered the same opinion. The following year, she was asked how many sitting-crawl steps she had done at the time – about 4, 10 or 20? About 10, she thought. If the exercise is found useful, it is probably best done just before bedtime.

### Awareness of dreaming

The energetic head teacher who claimed to sleep all night in the recommended position also said that he never dreamt. A mother who slept in position said she did not dream much. The possible reduction in awareness of dreaming was being mentioned to one parent, when her son excitedly interrupted to say that he used to dream a lot but 'now' he didn't.

### A child rocking and moaning when asleep

A boy (7yrs 10m) who was receiving support in a small group at school for reading began the sleeping work. His mother reported that he had almost stopped the moaning and rocking which 'for years now' had often disturbed them at three o'clock in the morning. It was a problem that the doctor had failed to help him with, but after beginning the sleeping routine the child had only moaned slightly about four times. On one such occasion mother found him still in the recovery position.

### A child coughing in the night

Another boy (8yrs 4m) had coughed a lot in the middle of the night before assistance with sleeping began. Medicines had been tried without success, but after the sleeping work began most of the coughing stopped.

### A child's involuntary neck stretching and eye movements

The doctor and head teacher allowed assistance to be given to a primary school boy with neck stretching and eye movements, both involuntary, done even when swimming; so he began the sleeping work, crawling and walking. Nine days later, the child had fallen asleep in position a few nights, but had come out of it very soon: in his mother's view, he was 'getting away nicely' with the exercises. On Day 2, she had not seen him do the involuntary movements, but on Day 3 (Saturday) father and mother, watching carefully, saw the movements only once. However, the involuntary movements reappeared when the boy decided that he couldn't fall asleep in that position (the easier step of morning rest in position had not begun).

Some of his switch-offs might have been so severe that his concentration flowed not only over to the pictures side but down into the brain-stem, where involuntary movements might be stimulated. Consequently, strengthening the brain-stem with the sleeping work and early motor development could well have enabled him to keep concentration on the words side, or at least on the pictures side without the involuntary movements.

These instances of benefit lead one to wonder what other implications there might be from the what is probably the main thrust of Delacato's theory.

# Chapter Thirteen

## An Initial Strategy For Parents And Teachers

### 1. The Special Needs Teacher

In Years 2 to 4, if 'c-a-t' type blends cannot be made although the most common sound of their letters are known to the child, have the child sit on a chair away from the gaze of other children. Ask the child to place his feet on the floor and lightly hold the front edge of the chair. As you count from one to six, he should try to lift slightly both one foot and the opposite hand on the count of two and return them to the original position on the count of four. Repeat the count as he moves the other pair of limbs similarly; then alternate these two 'steps'. Experience suggests that he will almost certainly fail quickly, to his surprise, and will wish to conquer the exercise. If so, ask him to join you in counting a series of one to six while he lifts one arm on the count of two and down on the count of four. He does it five times with each arm and each leg, one at a time, these movements forming level one of the sitting-crawl. Successive levels seen in Chapter 5 are tested until one is found which he can almost do – but not quite. It is suggested there how much work should be done at a particular level, so supervise him doing that amount at his threshold level and tell him to do exactly that each day until you check it the following week. When he succeeds at one level, he continues at successive levels until completing the original exercise at which he failed. Now, ask him to read a list of six three-letter words which can be sounded out but are uncommon, like the examples in Chapter 2 ('wig, jot, led' rather than 'pat, dog, bed'). If he cannot read five of these words easily, have him polish the sitting-crawl; he may have been moving up the levels before he was ready, so ensure that he performs well at the earlier stages.

During Years 5 to 8, generally variable performance which we associate with infants may linger. Usually, perhaps always, it will affect spelling, where its effect will be obvious. It is easy to overlook the high variability of an able child performing at average level in class, so it is safer to have each child screened as early as possible in Years 5 to 8 with a double mini-dictation. Children with 0% variability on the first mini-dictation are likely to have an average below 33% and may be eliminated. Children averaging 15% after the second dictation should be satisfactory, too. Successively test the children and eliminate those showing an average of 33% variability or less after three or four sessions.

Of the remaining few, plan to take two at a time. Select a pair who seem to be in the greatest need, considering their apparent difficulties in learning or behaviour, poor self-organisation and high variability of spelling. Initially, their parents should be informed about the background of the idea and the support which is available. Arrange a meeting with the parent or parents at home or school in which the programme is explained, tests of cross-pattern progression given and, if needed, remediation begun. This meeting should take about 40 minutes if a review is given out on loan.

After giving a brief outline of the idea, test the walking and crawling, which usually show some weakness, then explain a bit more of the theory, including the sleeping work – the most fundamental and most powerful part of all and the part which most parents eagerly seize upon. Begin the sleeping work with any walking and crawling exercises. If the walk is almost impossible, first try the sitting-crawl and later the stilted walk, pausing between each step. Similarly, if the crawl is exceedingly difficult, try the sitting-crawl followed in due course by the stilted crawl, raised limbs hanging between each step. The sleeping-turn may be demonstrated by the teacher standing on one leg against a door; the child usually learns it in three to 20 turns (see Figures 7 to 12). He begins by turning to the count of five, it quickly becoming a continuous movement with limbs and head moving at once.

The component parts of the programme are:

- Resting in position for 20 minutes each morning is introduced as 'important', and the other facets of the work are mentioned:
- slowness of sleeping-turn,
- evening rest in position (initially two minutes on each side),
- limit of ten minutes in position before sleep,

- sensible and regular bedtimes,
- staying up on Friday/Saturday limited to half an hour (again, this requirement is for the children with poor concentration),
- lack of excitement or study in the last half-hour before settling down to sleep,
- use of a thin pillow,
- nose off the edge of the pillow is recommended,
- exercises such as the cross-crawl, before bed, to eliminate superfluous energy, if necessary.

Particular problems may be discussed on the telephone when they crop up, like older sisters keeping the light on in the same bedroom till midnight while doing homework.

Parents will almost certainly agree to the procedure being monitored at school. For a few minutes each week, take the pair of children simultaneously in a carpeted room away from the idle curiosity of other children. Also, test the pair for variability of spelling. If the average of these scores remains above 33% after the early motor movements have been perfected, arrange for the child to wear a sling on the non-writing arm to strengthen the neural pathways to the writing hand. Ask that he wears it for ten minutes early each evening during a half-term: it gives the child a mind-set to keep the writing arm as the active one and normally produces a decrease in average variability of spelling. If the average variability remains over 33%, the child should use the sling for an hour on at least 15 evenings in another half-term; the earlier progress encourages the child to persevere in this more demanding task.

While he is doing the exercises and before the sudden surge of almost all-round progress, encourage him to use his handwriting hand (if clearly preferred and better) in those other one-handed activities where he is willing. The idea is that the more he can become one-sided, the more he is firming up the neural pathways to that hand (or foot or eye or ear) and the greater contribution he is making to achieving an early dominant channel. If he is right-sided in all four areas, so much the better. (A footballer using both feet about equally at this stage could be put on the right side of the field to use his right foot more, temporarily.) After achieving dominance with the dominant pathways set, he may choose to be ambidextrous. This instruction is easily forgotten and it is aggravating to find a couple of years later that a child making slower progress than anticipated is freely using both hands in single-handed activities.

It helps to keep together records of (1) sleeping work, exercises and use of the sling, and (2) average spelling variability of the previous three or four sessions, because progress with the second largely determines the emphasis placed on the first.

Most of those children can thus be helped in a fundamental way which will help all their learning and play: better to accept a reduced time to teach spelling than use all that time to push spelling into a child whose mind is constantly flitting on and off the work. In the case of the occasional child in whom variability remains high, see the section for parents about waiting three months before considering specialist help.

If poor spelling was the problem and a variability below 33% is now clearly established, encourage a renewed attitude to spelling. The child has to eradicate all those wrong impressions he has gained in the days of switching off frequently. Usually, it should be enough for him to look up needed words in a dictionary, and list them by subject or just by date. He should underline the difficult parts and read through the lists from time to time. However, sometimes, if spelling ability is particularly weak, a child might need a fresh course in spelling.

Ideally, children with a poor posture that allows the eyes to come close to the paper almost certainly would benefit from reflex development. Failing that, 'Sit up' is better than 'Head up,' for it results in the head staying up longer, and explaining the need to save his eyes will encourage the child's co-operation. For grip on pen or pencil, it is generally accepted that the important thing is for the index finger to guide it by lying approximately down the upper side of the implement.

## Parents

Ensure that the normal school checks on vision and hearing have been carried out. If you neither rest nor sleep in the recovery position, rest in it for 20 minutes before rising. Done over at least a few mornings, it will give you some idea of the benefit your child should obtain.

If this work is done at school, you will probably be glad to let the special needs teacher monitor the exercises at school, but be at the initial session with teacher and child. Supervise the set exercises as much as necessary, especially with the younger child. However, if the child's doziness varies considerably from day to day, please encourage the class teacher and, perhaps, other affected persons to take an interest in the child's sleeping work: at the very least, he should be become aware of its importance. If necessary, follow the special needs teacher's programme as much as you can yourself: remember the sling work on the non-writing arm comes last after the exercises which in theory strengthen the brain-stem have been perfected. However, at an early stage, as soon as you are sure which is clearly his better hand for writing, encourage him to do as many of his one-handed activities as possible with it.

Should switching off remain excessive, wait three months after the programme has been completed. If not satisfied with your child's concentration, and if his variability of spelling is 33% or above, he may need specialist help. This assistance may be with aberrant underlying reflexes (Chapter 11), with audiometric tests (Chapter 7), with tinted lenses (Chapters 7, 8) or with nutrition (Chapter 12). Many of the specialists listed in 'Addresses For Help With Reflexes' also do audiometric tests. No doubt, if there are problems in more than one area, tackling one problem well will make it less urgent to tackle the other problems, although ideally they should all be tackled. It seems that sorting out the reflexes in this way is a basic requirement, which if attended to will often greatly reduce or remove other problems. You can help your child in certain areas, particularly before he acquires his dominance, in these ways:

i.  If your child is driven to school, park 100 yards/metres away and encourage him to walk in briskly. Take other opportunities for him to walk at least that far.

ii. If your child when showing concentration problems tends to do two things at once, praise him when he attends well to one activity at a time.

iii. Expect your child to switch attention reasonably quickly from one thing to another when, for example, he has to come for a meal.

iv. Encourage your child to switch on maximum attention when needed, for example, before giving instructions – and do not impart vital details until he does so.


## 3. The Class Teacher

When a mainstream class teacher realises that a child is making more silly mistakes than usual, she may ask him privately and quietly about his sleeping work. Poor rest overnight seems to be the commonest cause of 'bad' days with children referred from mainstream education by an educational psychologist, and may apply to mainstream children in general. At secondary schools in particular, subject teachers could make a useful contribution, reinforcing for the child the good practice suggested in this section.

Was he late going to bed? If so, urge him to keep trying for a sensible bedtime. If he did not wake in position, did he rest in it for 20 minutes that morning? If not, urge him to remember to do it the next morning. If there is a problem with being woken in time, have a word with mother.

If not late the previous evening, was he late to bed recently and, if so, how much later was he than usual? The child should be reminded that 'bedtime' refers to settling down to sleep. Did he either watch exciting television or study in the last half-hour?

Was he more than half an hour later to bed the previous Friday and Saturday? Nearly always, the child admits to having slipped up on some part of the sleeping work. A calm, relaxed approach to the child works well and may be followed by a reminder when necessary.

At the very least, the teacher is reminding him of good sleeping habits which bring more 'good' days and fewer 'bad' days. Much experience suggests parents are always glad of co-operation with their child's sleeping if he has learning difficulties.

This regime can be relaxed at the approach of the summer holiday and at Christmas, for some days after a holiday, in times of illness, and when other conditions hinder comfortable working. These include surrounding noise and haste, poor lighting and ventilation, unsatisfactory ergonomics of desk and chair, poor view of the blackboard, head low to the paper provoking eyestrain, and weak vision and hearing. Help may be needed with these conditions, and comments above directed towards the special needs teacher on posture and pen grip also apply in mainstream classes.

# *Chapter Fourteen*

## Conclusion

The investigation with identical twins summarised in Chapter 3 tends to confirm the immediate value of resting in the recovery/ transformed tonic neck reflex position for 20 minutes. Whichever way the average variability scores are compared, the implication is the same: lying awake in position for that period seems to promote rest more than does lying on the back. Also, two women independently discovered the value of lying awake in position before rising for 20 and 15 minutes to be 'fit for work'; one was a deputy head teacher and the other became one. Parents in general have been quick to enthusiastically appreciate the sleeping work.

Rhythm tends to slot switch-off rest pauses in between chunks of work so that they cause less disturbance to learning; a second benefit is that less frustration encourages the child to try harder. In Chapter 10, reference was made to three children who showed not only benefit from the exercises, but a relapse when the exercises were given up, which suggests that the benefit had been real enough.

Sheila Dobie (1993) conducts a 'tour de force' of the support for both motor development and the role of reflexes in connection with SpLD (specific learning difficulties). With regard to the underlying reflexes, Mark Mathews and Elizabeth Thomas in Appendix 6 give impressive evidence showing the educational value of establishing them.

It seems that most children who have motor difficulties at six years have similar problems at sixteen years (Anna Losse *et al.* 1991). Thus, if it is thought that unsatisfactory early motor development might contribute to a child's difficulties, it should be remedied as soon as possible.

Posthumous examination of the brains of dyslexics has shown the corpus callosum, the band of fibres linking the two hemispheres, is enlarged. This enlargement is what one would expect of a person who had frequent, tiny switch-offs, so that concentration, as postulated in this book, flows backwards and forwards between the hemispheres repeatedly.

Perhaps the best test of a good concept is that in many related fields of study it makes sense. The idea based on Delacato's work offers some help in many areas of concern such as those in Chapter 12. However, the burden of proof is not too great, for family stress is not involved and special needs teachers spending some of their time on concentration work will find all their other work eased. Much can be achieved by simple exercises for a few minutes each day at home, with parents supervising top infants and younger juniors.

As a result of work on the physical basis of concentration, a lot of mainstream children with concentration problems should be happier, be more confident, benefit more from their time at school, and be more satisfied that they are fulfilling their potential. Standards in education ought to rise among those who need remedial help with concentration.

If we fail to assist them, some children might find it so hard to keep relating from the words side that they give up and spend their time on the more self-concerned side. Thus they might regard selfish behaviour as the norm, leading in the extreme case to a life of crime. It could be an early step in the rehabilitation of prisoners to teach them the sleeping position. Thoroughly rested, they should be able to stay on the language side of the brain more and relate better.

Both adults and children (NOT babies before they achieve the transformed tonic neck reflex) who practice the sleeping work should experience good rest for work and leisure. Morning rest in position is at least a partial substitute for a good night's rest and could be of widespread benefit.

## Further Research

If research is undertaken on brainwaves of people resting in the recovery/relaxation position, and if a comparison of these waves is made with those of subjects resting on their backs, one might expect that those in the recovery position would show the alpha rhythm of relaxation much sooner than those lying on their backs. Such a finding would have implications for settling to sleep as well as for a period of rest prior to rising.

An experiment could be done with children considered by an educational psychologist to have SpLD. A test such as the tapping test seen in Appendix 2 might be done before and shortly after 20 minutes' rest. It should show whether the recovery position or the supine position is better at reducing excessive switch-offs. Alternatively, an investigation such as that carried out with identical twins, mentioned in Chapter 3, might be carried out.

An advisory service offering flexible support for children with difficulties in the basic subjects or in concentration, or in both, would be more successful (i.e. more pleasing for children, teachers and parents) than any service tried so far and would not be too expensive. Also, special needs teachers and parents should be encouraged to 'have a go', because even bits of the programme such as walking, the sitting-crawl or the sleeping work often bring mainstream children with learning difficulties immediately into the normally teachable bracket.

# *Appendix 1*

## Attention Deficit Disorder (ADD)

Attention Deficit Disorder is usually associated with hyperactivity (ADD/H), but not everyone accepts that it might be linked to problems without hyperactivity (ADD/WO). Lahey and Carlson (1991) review the debate, claiming that there is evidence to support the distinction. The two types are discerned in DSM-111 (see note) but, in the revised DSM-111-R, the distinction was nearly omitted. However, a category 'Undifferentiated Attention Deficit Disorder' was finally added.

There can be two relevant results of a switch-off: (1) Stray topics brought back from the creative side of the brain might contribute to disruptive behaviour as seen in Appendix 4. (2) Confusions at and forgetting after a switch-off might result in adding to SpLD (specific learning difficulties). The stray topics could be a cause of ADD/H, and the confusions and forgetting a cause of ADD/WO.

Between these two extremes of either just stray topics (contributing to hyperactivity) or just confusions with forgetting (contributing to SpLD), there may be a scale on which a child with excessive switching off might be represented. So, if the explanation is correct, there may be a scale between just ADD/H and just ADD/WO on which a child's problem might be registered.

Children with ADD/H, ADD/WO or a combination of both should benefit from work on the physical basis of concentration. (It greatly helps a number of hyperactive children to have a nutritionally balanced diet avoiding foods to which they are intolerant.) Switch-offs ought to be fewer and the attention-stretch between them longer. Consequently, behaviour problems and learning difficulties should be reduced.

With regard to variability of performance, Hynd *et al.* (1989) found that the variability in two speeded tasks best showed the difference between the ADD/H group and the control group. They conclude that it might be better to refer to Variable Attention Disorder (VAD) rather than Attention Deficit Disorder. So, it seems that switch-offs, resulting in variable performance, might be a cause of ADD or 'VAD'.

**Notes:**

Reference reprinted from G.W. Hynd *et al.*, 'Attention Deficit Disorder with and without Hyperactivity: Reaction Time and Speed of Cognitive Processing', *Journal of Learning Disabilities*, Nov. 1989 , 573-80. Copyright 1989, by permission of the publisher Churchill Livingstone.

DSM refers to *Diagnostic and Statistical Manual of Mental Disorders*, (3rd ed., 1980; and Revised 4th ed., 1987) prepared and published by the American Psychiatric Association, Washington D.C., USA.

# *Appendix 2*

## Voluntary/Involuntary Aspects Of Switch-Offs

An experience similar to the switch-off in a child's attention might be experienced by the adult while choral singing. A word which appeared easy to predict might be misread but, with the benefit of immediate hindsight and sharpened attention, it becomes clear that the word had not registered.

One might almost think that by some process the brain unconsciously says to itself, 'Oh! This word is easy. I'll have a little rest.' Perhaps the brain tends to take control of its own switching off when the attention level is low; but when attention consciously sharpens, the will takes greater control.

More determination to pay attention is needed if, also, there is boredom, or distraction by thoughts or by environment. There is an interplay between the voluntary factor of willpower to attend and the involuntary factors of boredom, distraction and predictability. Therefore, the factors that govern a switch-off seem partly voluntary and partly involuntary: a switch-off may be regarded as a rest pause, usually momentary, over which one has only partial control.

### The Tapping Test

Much interesting work on involuntary rest pauses (IRPs), though not in this particular context, has been done by H. J. Eysenck and others. There can be little doubt that the same brain function is involved in the tiny switch-offs which have been considered.

A tapping test was used in which the person tested was required to tap as fast as possible for a minute. Eysenck, using apprentices of high-drive and low-drive motivation, found that comparing apprentices with an equal number of taps the high-drive group had fewer IRPs in a tapping test, just short of significance. This group thought that the tests might assist their entry to a training course which would further their career; the second group were tested after acceptance for the course.

Reproduced with permission of publisher from Eysenck, H. J., 'Involuntary rest pauses in tapping as a function of drive and personality', *Perceptual and Motor Skills*, 18, 1964,  173–74. © Southern Universities Press, USA.

Wilson, Tunstall and Eysenck (1972, p. 16) drew further attention to the finding about high-drive subjects tending to produce fewer IRPs.

 So, it appears that motivation might play a part in reducing IRPs; that rest pauses called involuntary may be partly voluntary. As mentioned, teachers rightly badger children to keep their attention on the task: they expect children, by their own efforts, to reduce the number of and extent of these momentary losses of attention.

A child with learning difficulties, however, may have frequent rest pauses which he cannot reduce enough. It seems clear that their frequency can be reduced by an initial approach of helping the involuntary aspect. A second approach must be for the child to make every effort himself to maintain attention. While a physical basis of concentration (if it is necessary to work on it) is being established, the child should still try hard to keep his attention 'on task'. The first approach might be needed – the second certainly is. When the physical basis of concentration and hemispheric dominance have been formed, the child's further development of attention obviously depends on his own will. Gradually, the support he needs from home and school dwindles.

# *Appendix 3*

## Right Hemisphere Before Left

In Chapter 2, it was suggested that the secure working of the right hemisphere develops before that of the left. In the particular area of reading, Professor Dirk Bakker (1990, 1995) appears of this opinion. (He, too, takes the case of language residing in the left hemisphere.)

Bakker (1990) states that reading, at first, mainly needs 'a perceptual analysis of the form and direction of letters and words', which is best done by the right hemisphere. The left hemisphere is primarily linguistic and works best 'when the perceptual features of the text no longer require much attention'.

Up to 60% of dyslexics have been classified as L- or P-types. P-dyslexics get off to a good start using right-hemisphere strategies but do not progress to left-hemisphere strategies. L-dyslexics get off to a wrong start with left-hemisphere strategies.

'The L-dyslexics would be the *relatively* fast-inaccurate readers and the P-dyslexics the *relatively* slow-accurate ones.' McFarlane Smith (1964), noting four others, and Sweeney and Rourke (1985) also differentiated between readers with these characteristics. Bakker planned to help the former by stimulating the right hemisphere and the latter by the left hemisphere.

Of the L-dyslexics in five groups, the two which were experimental both showed better average progress in a word recognition test and in a sentence reading test than did the three control groups.

Of the five groups of P-dyslexics, however, the children in one control group recorded, on average, the best scores in the two tests. For this group, both hemispheres were stimulated: the right, visually, by perceptually laden text using a mixture of typefaces;

the left by rhyming and temporal sequencing. That is to say, the child gave a rhyming word to complete a couplet and then related the sounds of the word in order.

The success of this control group might be explained if the P-type dyslexic has a low level of concentration overall: perhaps both sides of the brain have to be targeted to stimulate their activity.

If Bakker is correct for the L-type dyslexic in seeing the need to stimulate the right hemisphere, he may be correct for the L-type child in general. The quick and careless child might have missed some early development of his visual side: possibly his art and music need extra attention.

It might be that this is the kind of child whose reading is aided by occasionally turning the book upside down: perhaps it makes him look more carefully and use the visual hemisphere more. Poor visual discrimination might be a problem here, too, when learning key sight words: it certainly seems to be another common cause of frustration.

If either type of dyslexic has poor concentration, it is likely to involve excessive switching off, probably affecting spelling. The apparently accelerated lowering of a high variability of spelling should show the benefit of the Delacato-type work.

# *Appendix 4*

## Behaviour Difficulties

On the one hand, the child with learning difficulties may find switching off causes confusions, reversals and, on switching back in, loss of immediate memory. On the other hand, the child with behaviour difficulties may be affected differently by switch-offs. At the non-confrontational stage, he may bring back stray topics from the creative side of the brain: 'I can't wait for tonight'; 'There's something on the floor'; or 'He's not getting on with his work'. We can think of switch-offs as contributing to both problems, often seen with the same child.

Alternatively, an urge brought in from the poorer-relating, more self-concerned side of the brain might be to wander round the classroom looking for an escape interest. It might be a bit like an adult escaping in a book at bedtime. When tired we, too, often seek a break from disciplined perception and response.

The parent of a boy who had been helped at the Remedial Centre was teaching at a local high school. The head of Year 9 asked her to assist in her own time with a disruptive boy who, for example, climbed on desks. She saw him at break-time and lunch-time. Her son, also at the school, showed him the sleeping position, walking and crawling, and she monitored his progress. Behaviour was noticeably better but it tended to regress when the exercises were given up. Then he joined a group for remedial work where the head of department was pleased to find that he was determined to progress out of it.

The tiredness may not be obvious: the restless behaviour may be due to a hidden lack of rest. With such children, only when the sleeping work begins does one see the improvement it can bring. The co-operation the child generally brings to the sleeping routine as well as the exercises is particularly appreciated when working with a disruptive child; perhaps he feels a basic need is satisfied by this work.

A disruptive infant in a class of twelve at a centre for disturbed mainstream children threw a broken bottle over a fence, put a letter down a drain, and pulled at the teacher's jerkin zip, breaking it. He was shown the sleeping position and seven days later was reported as 'much better behaved this week' – perhaps chance, but his willingness to accept the teaching suggests a possible course of action in such circumstances.

One boy had finished his course at the Remedial Centre including walking, crawling and monitoring of sleep. His secondary school remedial teacher (later a primary school head teacher) reported a 'big effect' on his aggressiveness in class as well as a 'marked improvement' in his work.

A Year 3 boy was doing the sleeping work, with a nearly perfect sitting-crawl and frog-wriggle, for restless and irritating behaviour. One day the head teacher telephoned to say how disturbing the boy had been. After his mother received the message, she excitedly reported that neither in the morning nor in the previous evening had he done the usual sleeping routine or exercises. Organisation, however, was not a strong point at his home.

Over 20 years ago, on a second visit to Winchester, it was astonishing to be greeted by the head teacher with the question: 'Do you think that children should be allowed to sleep in school?' This question is not such a strange one, for, when driving far, it is surprising how a break with a short nap helps one to stay switched in for a considerable time. Also, in many Japanese firms 15 minutes' rest is thought to be as good as a sleep of four hours. And there is even a sleeping room in the House of Commons. Perhaps erratic behaviour is often due to a tired child withdrawing his concentration from the task and allowing it to switch over to the more self-concerned side of the brain, in a similar way to that suggested in 'Feeling warm and cool towards others', described in Chapter 12.

Sometimes a disruptive child is sent to stand outside the classroom to calm down when he really needs effective rest. Instead, the child might be sent to rest in position for, say, 20 minutes in a quiet room with an adult in sight. It is worth trying this, for the improvement in behaviour could be remarkable. Before returning to class, the child should be reminded to do his sleeping work, for the more prompts he receives about this work the better.

There is another, less fundamental solution to the problem of excessive switching off. Instead of reducing switch-offs, one can make the best of them by neutralising their disturbing effect as follows.

## Lost Concentration Occupied by Classical Music

Shown on BBC1's 'Watchdog Healthcheck', Monday 2-2-98, the children in Anne Savan's science lesson, Aberdare Boys Comprehensive School, had severe behavioural problems, but were silent and got on with the lesson when calming and pleasant classical music was played in the background. In an experiment, the group taught with this music playing showed lower pulse rate, blood pressure and body temperature after 20 minutes (Savan 1998). In another study, Dr. Susan Hallam, psychologist at the Institute of Education, tested the ability to solve mathematics problems while listening to such music; the experimental group performed better. She has added that there were two studies of upper junior children showing the same result, one group from a mainstream school and the other from a school for children with emotional and behavioural difficulties. Interestingly, one possible explanation given in the programme was that, 'if they lost concentration for a moment, then it was taken up by listening to the music and then they immediately turned back to doing the maths' (Price and Hallam 1997).

This idea fits with that expressed here: if attention switches off for a moment, concentration largely flows to the subdominant and tonal side of the brain; reversals, confusions and stray topics are normally returned to the language side as attention is re-established. However, in the above case, the music tends to occupy concentration in the subdominant hemisphere, causing less disruption to the child's relating.

# *Appendix 5*

## Marking The Variable Spelling Test

The following detail is an attempt to form as nearly as possible a standard test of variable spelling. The child's reading book is used, taking a passage not yet read on the day or, if necessary, an unread portion. He is given a mini-dictation from a text which is difficult enough for five or six countable errors to be made within approximately 20 to 40 words. A text at about instructional level (where an average of 19 out of 20 words can be read) is usually suitable.

Within half a minute or so, a repeat 'dictation' begins in which the child tries to produce the same spellings. Even when a misspelling in the first dictation is remembered correctly in the second dictation, he should remember the error and record that again. If a word is omitted the first time, it should be left out the next time too. He is regularly told until he knows not to improve the spelling the second time, and children pick up the idea readily enough.

Proper nouns are discounted, including names such as Tom King and His Majesty, as well as days and months to be consistent. Words like 'blackboard' written by the child as two words are marked as one word; and vice versa when two words are required. Elisions are removed ('she is' rather than 'she's') to avoid that complication. Apostrophes, capital letters and other punctuation are not scored.

At least 60% of the letters of the correct word must occur in the correct order for corresponding words in both dictations. If not, the word is considered too difficult and both errors are disregarded. If a word, however, such as 'convict' is correct in one dictation but is shown as, say, 'kondic' in the other, the error is regarded as a variable one even though less than 60% of the letters occur in the correct order.

When an error is the same in both dictations, it rates as two 'fixed' errors. When an error is repeated differently, two 'variable' errors are recorded. If an error-pair recurs the same, the second pair is ignored: if there is any difference in the recurring pair, it is scored separately.

An omitted word is rated as a variable error, but the corresponding word in the other dictation, if correct or having too few letters in the correct order, as in 'sir/she', is ignored. If a word is omitted on both occasions, the first is regarded as a variable error and the second as a fixed error. A word may be omitted in one dictation (and counted variable), but recorded wrongly in the other. The latter is counted a variable error if at least 60% of the correct letters occur in the correct order.

Inserted words are also rated as variable errors unless the same in both dictations: in the latter case the first is considered variable and the second fixed. Letters inserted in a word are ignored, to avoid complication, when calculating the percentage of letters represented in the correct order; but they do count towards a variable spelling as in 'the'/'the, ther' and towards fixed errors as in 'are'/'arer, arer', where 'arer' is written in both dictations for 'are'.

If the child's 'a/o' or other letter pairs are confusable, the child is asked which is intended. The child is allowed no alteration for change of spelling: the word is rewritten (although attention is sharpened and errors often corrected, clarity is important for marking). So, writing on alternate lines is advisable. Only b/d confusions are ignored, for they are so common, appearing to be easily confused. Uncrossed 't's have been counted but undotted 'i's have not seemed a problem. Fortunately, debatable errors are rare and little affect the impression of variability averaged over 20 or more errors on three or four sessions. A stroke leading off the top of a 'u' is allowed if consistent, but not otherwise.

The switch-offs are really just moments of appreciably lowered attention liable to cause variable errors. In one case, three consecutive words were wrong in one dictation but correct in the other – words in the region were correct. It appeared to be one longer switch-off, so that a score of three variable errors gave a fair indication of the problem.

Average variabilities may be calculated for comparison: variable errors over a few double mini-dictations are added up and divided by the total number of variable and fixed errors, leaving out disregarded errors. Conveniently expressed as a percentage, the average variability gives a useful impression of the frequency of switch-offs in spelling. It is simplest to compare the average variability during groups of three or four sessions.

A score of 100% variability suggests much switching off, while 0% implies well-maintained attention. The increase of a middling score probably means an increased amount of switching off, although probably not in a linear relationship. One argument to support this suggestion is a comparison with a shower of rain. When a light shower becomes heavier more of the path is hit: similarly, if the switch-offs 'raining down' on words of which the child is unsure become more frequent, then more of these words will be 'hit' and are likely be altered.

By its nature the test cannot be entirely reliable. For '... not going to let a hare outpace him', one child produced 'nat gowing to let a hair out pest Him' and then 'nat gowing to let a hair out peyst Him.' His spelling of 'outpace' was marked as one word because of the original text. It had enough letters in the correct order for each to count, so they made two variable errors. Had the word been ordered the word as 'out pace', his 'out' would have been correct and his 'pace' would not have counted. Despite such problems, the test averages can distinguish between children scoring high and low, which is useful provided individual circumstances are taken into account.

For initial testing, the class requires a passage which tests the best spellers (who might also show a high variability). As the text will be difficult for the weaker spellers, the teacher moving around should stop them as soon as possible after their five or six countable errors. As children with low variability are gradually removed, the problem becomes less and a group of children needing help are selected. Texts of gradually increasing difficulty would be helpful for the initial screening tests.

When beginning to work with pairs of children, short portions of say 11 to 14 words from each of their reading books may be dictated to both children. Words not clear to the tester should be rewritten. About ten seconds might be allowed for children to look through their first dictation before, say, folding their A4 sheet and beginning their repeat dictation. The original text has to be borrowed or jotted down for marking later: the rhythm of the lesson seems spoilt if marking of both scripts is attempted at the time.

# *Appendix 6*

## Results Of Reflexes

Work on aberrant reflexes may be just part of the work offered by a centre. For example, in Applied Kinesiology for learning difficulties, it is claimed that the whole child is studied, including a great many reflexes. For this approach a trained osteopath does a further part-time postgraduate training at the International College for Applied Kinesiology.

Mark Mathews assists children, who are tested before and after by Elizabeth Thomas, educational psychologist. She has a private practice assisting children with specific learning difficulties.

In one investigation ten children in the treatment group were matched with ten in a control group. The latter were given similar exercises, but which were not diagnosed for them. The gains of the first group compared with the second were impressive in visual sequencing, visual discrimination, construction, copying and short-term memory. The most significant improvement was a gain of 70% as against 20% for the control group; least impressive, but still good, was an improvement of 30% by the treatment group compared with 20% for the controls.

The average gain in IQ of the treatment group was eight points. The gains were 12 on the performance scale and three on the verbal scale. There was a slight negative progress in the control group of the average quotient and the performance scale.

One child in the treatment group had an IQ of 70 to 75. He was diagnosed as suffering from lead poisoning. After treatment, his spelling age leapt by 19 months in nine months. One might suggest that dominance had been gained.

In another experiment, the IQ of the 12 in the treatment group again rose by eight points. This time the verbal ability improved more than the performance ability.

Much of this information is recorded in *A Pilot Study on the Value of Applied Kinesiology in Helping Children with Learning Disabilities*, produced by The Rêve Pavilion, 2a Guildford Park Road, Guildford, Surrey.

# Addresses For Help With Reflexes

The following centres and individuals work wholly or partly with Specific Learning Difficulties, and include varied work on reflex development or related work. The letters in brackets after a specialist's name indicate that a course of training has been completed at The Institute For Neuro-Physiological Psychology (INPP), or at the Centre for Developmental Learning Difficulties (CDLD) which operated until recently.

The INPP, as explained, employ exercises to eliminate primitive reflexes which should have been extinguished. On the other hand, the CDLD employed brushing to eliminate reflexes which should have been extinguished before birth (an artist's type of brush sufficed). One hears that brushing had a beneficial 'knock on' effect upon the primitive reflexes, but, if necessary, they used exercises to eliminate the remaining unwanted reflexes.

A recently formed group which includes Krystyna Proctor are among those giving much attention to developing this work. They plan to explain their Developmental Integration Therapy in a book shortly. It should be noted that occupational therapists also use a kind of brushing, but for quite a different reason. Seemingly OTs reduce tactile sensitivity, rather than inhibit developmental reflexes, employing brushes with different filaments and cloths of various textures.

Some specialists are qualified in more than one school of practice, so readers may expect specialists, at present, to employ exercises or brushing or both.


## 1. Work on Reflexes

The following practitioners offered services at the time of publication. All addresses UK unless otherwise stated.

Bob Allen, Jenn Clarke and Maureen Kirby (CDLD)
96 Clarence Road, Windsor, Berks SL4 5AT Tel: 01753 856100

Bob Allen (CDLD), 111 West Street, Farnham, Surrey GU9 7HH
Tel: 01420 520525

Pauline Allen (INPP), The Sound Learning Centre, 12 The Rise
London N13 5LE Tel: 0181 882 1060

Mary Atkinson (INPP), The Maypole Centre, Maypole Cottage
Bird Lane, Upminster, Essex RM14 1TY  Tel: 01708 221224

Elizabeth Ayres (INPP), 10 Betchton Road, Malkins Bank
Sandbach, Cheshire CW11 4XL Tel: 01270 760414

Edward Blackmore-Thomas (INPP), 34 Bedford Road, Rushden
Northants NN10 0NB Tel: 01933 318832

Peter Blythe and Sally Goddard Blythe, The Institute For Neuro-
Physiological Psychology (INPP), Warwick House, 4 Stanley Place
Chester CH1 2LU Tel/Fax: 01244 311414

Fioretta M. Blyde (INPP), Springfield, 13 Long Road
Cambridge CB2 2PP Tel: 01223 247203

Joan Brier (INPP), 60 Queensway, Moorgate, Rotherham
South Yorks S60 3EE Tel: 01709 362701

Lynne Bullerwell, Developmental Integration, 'Farthings',
Tanners Lane, Chalkhouse Green, Nr. Reading, Berks RG4 9AD
Tel: 0118 972 3979

Paul Burnett, Developmental Integration, 240 Hawes Lane
West Wickham, Kent BR4 9AQ Tel: 0181 776 2536 (several
locations)

Janet Chapman (INPP), 58 Penlon, Menai Bridge, Anglesey
LL59 5NE Tel: 01248 716170

Melvyn R. Clarke (INPP), Westfield Farm, The Courtyard Clinic
Coopers Hill, Eversley, Hants RG27 0QA Tel/Fax: 01252 870199

Debbie Cole (CDLD) and Colleen Reardon (CDLD),
2 Runnymede Gardens, Whitton, Twickenham, Middlesex
TW2 7BS Tel: 0181 898 4608

Peter Cousins (CDLD), 284 Broadway, Bexleyheath, Kent DA6
8AJ  Tel: 0181 303 6288/9571

Max Dale, Developmental Consultant (INPP & CDLD), The Max
Dale Centre of Reflex Development, 10 Woodside Road,
Chiddingfold, Surrey GU8 4UH Tel: 01428 685137;
also The Grove Centre, 22 Grosvenor Road, Highfield,
Southampton SO17 1RT Tel: 01703 582245;
also The Horsham Centre, 5A Park Place, Horsham RH12 1DF
Tel: 01403 271129

Sheila M. Dobie (INPP), The Institute for Neuro-Physiological
Psychology (Scotland), Centre for Sport and Exercise, University
of Edinburgh, Community Activities, Cramond Road North,
Edinburgh EH4 6JD Tel: 0131 312 6001

Mike and Helen Downey (INPP), The St. Briavels Centre for
Child Development, Dixton Road, Monmouth, Gwent NP5 3PR
Tel: 01600 713822

Frances Emmett (INPP), Little Parmoor Farm, Frieth
Henley on Thames, Oxon RG9 6NL Tel: 01494 881600

Jane Field (INPP), Gatepiece Cottage, Highfields, Wichenford
Worcestershire WR6 6YG Tel: 01886 888320

Elizabeth Franklin (INPP), 32 Rushbrook Avenue, Templeogue
Dublin 6W, Republic of Ireland Tel: (00 353 1) 450 2669

Gill Geraerts (INPP), The Therapy Centre, 1 Walkers Close
Harpenden, Herts AL5 1QJ Tel: 01582 765586

Hilary Green (INPP), Sunny Bank, Churchill, Chipping Norton
Oxon OX7 6NW Tel: 01608 659746

Christopher J. Guy (INPP), The Old Gaol, Broad Street
Long Compton, Warwickshire CV36 5JH Tel: 01608 684324

Andrew Holden (INPP), 6 Perth Road, Birnam, Dunkeld
Perthshire PH8 0DN Tel: 01350 727649

Alison Lawson (INPP), 5 Crocus Way, Simons Park, Wokingham
Berks RG41 3NW Tel: 0118 977 5204

Brenda Lloyd (INPP), 7 Heol-y-twyn, Pontlliw, Swansea
West Glamorgan SA4 1EU Tel: 01792 883855

Jessica Lough (INPP), 15 Boscombe Road, London W12 9HS
Tel: 0181 248 3939

Mark Mathews (see Appendix 6), Natural Health Clinic, The
Rêve Pavilion, Guildford Park Road, Guildford, Surrey GU2 5AD
Tel: 01483 579500

Pru Miller, Developmental Integration, Lyemarsh Farmhouse,
Wet Lane, Mere, Wiltshire BA12 6BA Tel: 01747 861330

David Mulhall, Developmental Consultant (INPP & CDLD)
David Mulhall Centre for Learning Difficulties, 16 Frewin Road
Wandsworth, London SW18 3LP Tel: 0181 877 3329

Jayne Nelson (INPP), 1 Crossways, Rookery Lane, Wendens
Ambo Saffron Walden, Essex CB11 4JR Tel: 01799 540404

Brian Newton (INPP), 44 Cuxton Close, Strelly, Nottingham
NG8 6LQ

Mary O'Connor (INPP), Balrickard, Galway Road, Headford
Co. Galway, Republic of Ireland Tel: (00 353) 93 35513

Lynne Pardoe (INPP), Kinloss School, Martley, Worcs WR9 7DF
Tel: 01886 888 223 (Ext. 28) Centre takes outside clients

Keith Phillips (INPP), 15 Mendham Way, Clophill, Bedford
MK45 4AL Tel: 01525 860616

Barbara Percy (INPP), 48 High Clere, Bewdley, Worcestershire
DY12 2EY Tel: 01299 401007

Krystyna Proctor, Developmental Integration, 39 Belton Grove
Grantham, Lincs, NG31 9HH Tel: 01476 593588

Patrick Reade (INPP), 10 Germander Close, Church Grange
Liverpool L26 7AJ Tel: 0151 487 9151

Gail Saye (INPP), The Lodge, Allcannings, Devizes, Wilts
SN10 3NR Tel: 01380 860756

Muriel Wall (INPP), St. Laurence House, 2 Gridiron Place
Upminster, Essex RM14 2BE Tel: 01708 641487

Gwen Wilkinson (INPP), Specific Learning Difficulty Centre
2 Lemontree Lane, Loughborough, Leics LE11 2QS
Tel: 01509 211281

Anne Willoughby (INPP), Tollgate House, 53 Lowgate Street
Eye, Suffolk IP23 7AT Tel: 01379 870298

Fran Woolgrove (INPP), Thirlestane House, Yetholm, Kelso
TD5 8PD Tel: 01573 420695

## 2. Work Relating to Reflexes

David Crawford and Sheila Crouch, Educational Kinesiology
(Brain Gym), 24 Fulwell Park Avenue, Twickenham, Middlesex
TW2 5HQ  Tel: 0181 898 0670

Educational Kinesiology U.K. Foundation (Brain Gym),
12 Golders Rise, Hendon, London NW4 2HR Tel: 0181 202 9747

Karen Lane, Knowle Hall, Knowle, Bridgewater, Somerset TA7
8PJ Tel: 01278 684060

## An Information Centre Covering a Wide Range of Childhood Problems

Gill Gleeson, The Rescue Foundation, Pigeonsford, Llangrannog
Llandysul, Ceredigion SA44 6AF Tel: 01239 654144 / 654983

# References

Excerpts from Dr. Carl H. Delacato in *Treatment and Prevention of Reading Problems* (1959), *Diagnosis and Treatment of Speech and Reading Problems* (1963), and *Neurological Organisation and Reading* (1966) are reproduced by courtesy of Charles C. Thomas, Publisher, Springfield, Illinois.

Bakker, Dirk J.: *Neuropsychological Treatment of Dyslexia* Copyright © 1990 by the publisher, Oxford University Press, Inc. Material reprinted with permission.

Mello, Nancy K.: "Concerning the Inter-Hemispheric Transfer of Mirror-Image Patterns in Pigeon." *Physiology and Behaviour* Vol.1, pp. 293–300. Copyright © 1966 by the publisher, Elsevier Science. Material reprinted with permission.

Rider, Barbara; "Relationship of Postural Reflexes to Learning Disabilities." *American Journal of Occupational Therapy* 26(5), pp. 239–243. Copyright © 1972 by the publisher, American Occupational Therapy Association, Inc. Material reprinted with permission.

The section on the sitting-crawl is taken, with some alterations, from the Newsletter (Spring, 1983) of the National Association of Remedial Education (NARE), now part of the National Association for Special Educational Needs (NASEN), with permission.

# Bibliography

American Academy of Pediatrics (1968). "The Doman-Delacato Treatment Of Neurologically Handicapped Children." *Journal Of Pediatrics*, 72, *May*, 750–52.

Anderson, R. Y. (1977). "Reading Forum No. 3: Helpful Ideas On Developing Concentration." *National Association Of Remedial Education Newsletter*, *Spring*, 4–5.

Anderson, R. Y. (1983). "Auditory Blending And The 'Sitting Crawl'." *National Association Of Remedial Education Newsletter*, *Spring*, 12–13.

Anderson, R. Y. (1996). *The Effect On Spelling Variability Of Rest In Two Different Positions With Possible Implications For The Sleeping Work*. 5 St. Celia's Way, Morecambe, Lancs.

Anderson, R. Y. (1997). *Establishing A Physical Basis Of Concentration In Identical Twins Monitored By Their Variability Of Spelling*. 5 St. Celia's Way, Morecambe, Lancs.

Bakker, D. J. (1990). *Neuropsychological Treatment Of Dyslexia*. Oxford: Oxford University Press.

Bakker, D. J., Licht, R. and Kappers, E. J. (1995). "Hemispheric Stimulation Techniques In Children With Dyslexia." *Advantages in Child Neuropsychology: Volume 3*, Eds. M. G.Tramontana and S. R. Cooper. New York: Springer-Verlag.

Berard, G. (1993). *Hearing Equals Behaviour*. New Canaan, Connecticut: Keats Publ. Inc.

Blythe, P. (1990). *The History Of The Institute for Neuro-Physiological Psychology (INPP)*. 4 Stanley Place, Chester: Institute Of Neuro-Physiological Psychology.

Blythe, P. (1992). *A Physical Approach To Resolving Learning Difficulties*. 4 Stanley Place, Chester: Institute for Neuro-Physiological Psychology.

Carlton, S. (1993). *The Other Side Of Autism: A Positive Approach*. Units 7/10 Hanley Workshops, Hanley Rd., Hanley Swan, Worcester: The Self Publishing Association Ltd.

Delacato, C. H. (1959). *The Treatment And Prevention Of Reading Problems*. Illinois: C. C.Thomas.

Delacato, C. H. (1963). *The Diagnosis And Treatment Of Speech And Reading Problems*. Illinois: C. C.Thomas.

Delacato, C. H. (1966). *Neurological Organisation And Reading*. Illinois: C. C.Thomas.

Delacato, C. H. (1974). *The Ultimate Stranger: The Autistic Child*. PO Box 1, Belford, Northumberland: Ann Arbor Publishers Ltd.

Delacato, C. H. (1982). *A New Start For The Child With Reading Problems*, 3rd Ed. Pennsylvania: Morton Books.

Dennison, P. E. and G. E. (1994). *Brain Gym: Teachers' Edition, Revised*. Ventura, California: Edu-Kinesthetics.

Dobie, S. (1993). "Perceptual Motor And Neuro-Developmental Dimensions In Identifying And Remediating Developmental Delay In Children With Specific Learning Difficulties." *Specific Learning Difficulties (Dyslexia): Perspectives On Practice*, Ed. G. Reid. Edinburgh: Moray House Publications.

Eysenck, H. J. (1964). "Involuntary Rest Pauses In Tapping As A Function Of Drive And Personality." *Perceptual And Motor Skills, 18, 1964*, 173–74.

Field, J. (1989). *Helping Specific Learning Difficulties By Correcting Underlying Physical Causes*. Gatepiece Cottage, Highfields, Wichenford, Worcestershire.

Field, J. (1990). *Talking To Teachers*. Gatepiece Cottage, Highfields, Wichenford, Worcestershire.

Field, J. (1992). *Your Vision Is Perfect: 'Why Don't You See?'* Gatepiece Cottage, Highfields, Wichenford, Worcestershire.

Field, J. (1995). *A Brief Description Of Some Reflexes Assessed In Neuro-Developmental Work.* Gatepiece Cottage, Highfields, Wichenford, Worcestershire.

Field, J. and Blythe, P. (1995). *Towards Developmental Re-Education.* Gatepiece Cottage, Highfields, Wichenford, Worcestershire.

Foresight. (1998). *Foresight Newsletter.* 28 The Paddock, Godalming, Surrey GU7 1XD.

Goddard, S. (1990). *A Developmental Basis For Learning Difficulties And Language Disorders.* 4 Stanley Place, Chester: Institute for Neuro-Physiological Psychology.

Goddard, S. (1991). *The Foundations For Life And For Living: An Introduction For Parents And Teachers.* 4 Stanley Place, Chester: Institute for Neuro-Physiological Psychology.

Goddard, S. (1996). *A Teacher's Window Into The Child's Mind And Papers From The Institute for Neuro-Physiological Psychology:* A Non-Invasive Approach to Solving Learning & Behaviour Problems. Oregon: Fern Ridge Press. 4, Stanley Place, Chester: Institute for Neuro-Physiological Psychology.

Goddard Blythe, S. and Hyland, D. (1998). "Screening For Neurological Dysfunction In The Specific Learning Difficulty Child." *The British Journal of Occupational Therapy,* October, 459–64.

Gold, S. J. (1986). *When Children Invite Child Abuse: A Search For Answers When Love Is Not Enough.* Oregon: Fern Ridge Press.

Gold, S. J. (1996). *Attention Deficit Syndrome: Educational Bugaboo Of The 90s.* 1927 McLean Blvd, Eugene, OR 97405, USA.

Hannaford, C. (1995). *Smart Moves: Why Learning Is Not All In Your Head.* Arlington, Virginia: Great Ocean Publishers.

Harris, D. A., and MacRow-Hill, S. J. (1998). "A Comparative Study With The Intuitive Colorimeter: Interim Report On The Use Of ChromaGen Contact Lenses In Patients With Specific Learning Difficulties." *Optometry Today, Vol. 38, July,* 15.

Hulme, C. and Bradley, L. (1984). "An Experimental Study Of Multi-Sensory Teaching With Normal And Retarded Readers." *Dyslexia: A Global Issue*, Eds. R. N. Malatesha and H. A. Whitaker. The Hague, Boston and Lancaster, PA USA: Martinus Nijhoff.

Hynd, G. W., Nieves, N., Connor, R. T., Stone, P., Town, P., Becker, M. G., Lahey, B. B. and Lorys, A. R. (1989). "Attention Deficit Disorder With And Without Hyperactivity: Reaction Time And Speed Of Cognitive Processing." *Journal Of Learning Disabilities*, November, 573–80.

Irlen, H. (1991). *Reading By The Colors: Overcoming Dyslexia And Other Reading Disabilities Through The Irlen Method*. New York: Avery.

Johansen, K. V. (1993). "Differential Diagnosis And Differentiated, Neuropsychological Treatments Of Dyslexia." *Legasthenie*, *October 1994*. (Hannover. Article also from Baltic Dyslexia Research Lab., Roe Skolevej 14, DK-3760 Gudhjem, Denmark.)

Lahey, B. B. and Carlson, C. L. (1991). "Validity Of The Diagnostic Category Of Attention Deficit Disorder Without Hyperactivity: A Review Of The Literature." *Journal Of Learning Disabilities*, *Feb*ruary, 110–20.

Losse, A., Henderson, S. E., Elliman, D., Hall, D., Knight, E. and Jongmans, M. (1991). "Clumsiness In Children: Do They Grow Out Of It? A 10-Year Follow-Up Study." *Developmental Medicine And Child Neurology*, 33, 55-68.

McGlown, D. (1990). *Developmental Reflexive Rehabilitation*. New York & London: Taylor & Francis.

Madaule, P. (1994). *When Listening Comes Alive: A Guide To Effective Learning And Communication*. Norval, Ontario, Canada: Moulin.

Manners, D. (undated). *Music To The Ears: Tomatis Method Case Studies*. Lewes, East Sussex: Tomatis Centre UK Ltd.

Masland, R. L. (1981). "Neurological Aspects Of Dyslexia." *Dyslexia Research And Its Applications To Education*, Eds. G. T. Pavlidis and T. R. Miles. Chichester and New York: Wiley & Sons.

Mello, N. K. (1966). "Concerning The Inter-Hemispheric Transfer Of Mirror-Image Patterns In Pigeon." *Physiology And Behaviour*, *1*, 293–300.

Miles, T. (1990). "Towards An Overall Theory Of Dyslexia." *Meeting Points In Dyslexia*, Eds. G. Hales, M. Hales, T. Miles and A. Summerfield. Reading: British Dyslexia Association.

Newton, M. (1970). "A Neuro-Psychological Investigation Into Dyslexia." *Assessment And Teaching Of Dyslexic Children*, Eds. A. W. Franklin and S. Naidoo. London: Invalid Children's Aid Association.

O'Dell, N. and Cook, P. (1977). *Stopping Hyperactivity: A New Solution. A Unique And Proven Program Of Crawling Exercises For Overcoming Hyperactivity*. New York: Avery.

Orton, S. T. (1925). "'Word-Blindness' in School Children." *Archives Of Neurology And Psychiatry*, *November*, 581–615.

Orton, S. T. (1937). *Reading, Writing And Speech Problems In Children*. London: Chapman & Hall.

Pavlidis, G. T. (1981). "Sequencing, Eye Movements And The Early Objective Diagnosis Of Dyslexia." *Dyslexia Research And Its Application To Education*, Eds. G. T. Pavlidis and T. R. Miles. Chichester & New York: Wiley & Sons.

Price, J. and Hallam, S. (1997). *Can Listening To Background Music Improve Children's Behaviour And Performance In Mathematics?* University of London: Institute of Education.

Pumphrey P. D. and Reason, R. (1991). *Specific Learning Difficulties (Dyslexia): Challenges And Responses*. Windsor: N.F.E.R.-Nelson.

Pyfer, J. L. (1998). "Teachers, Don't Let Your Students Grow Up To Be Clumsy Adults." *JOPERD*, *January*, 38–42.

Rider, B. (1972). "Relationship Of Postural Reflexes To Learning Disabilities." *American Journal of Occupational Therapy*, 26, 5, 239–43

Savan, A. (1998). "Study Of The Effect Of Background Music On The Behaviour And Physiological Responses Of Children With Special Educational Needs." *British Psychological Society Education Review*, *February*.

Smith, I. M. (1964). *Spatial Ability*. London: University of London Press.

Springer, S. P. and Deutsch, G. (1993, 4th ed.). *Left Brain, Right Brain*. Oxford: W. H. Freeman.

Sweeney, J. A. and Rourke, B. P. (1985). "Spelling Disability Subtypes." *Neuropsychology Of Learning Disabilities*, Ed. B. P. Rourke. London and New York: Guilford Press, 147–66.

Vitale, B. M. (1982). *Unicorns Are Real: A Right-Brained Approach To Learning*. California: Jalmer Press.

Wilkinson, G. J. (1994). "The Relationship Of Primitive Postural Reflexes To Learning Difficulty And Underachievement." Unpublished submission for M.Ed., School of Ed., University, Newcastle upon Tyne.

Wilson, G. D., Tunstall, O. A. and Eysenck, H. J. (1972). "Measurement Of Motivation In Predicting Industrial Performance: A Study Of Apprentice Gas Fitters." *Occupational Therapy*, 46, 15–24.

*Audio tape*: *A New Approach To Learning Difficulties*. WLAP (Wendy Lloyd Audio Productions) Ltd., PO Box 1, Wirral, Merseyside.

# Glossary

**Attention:** Attention is regarded as the outcome when concentration-flow builds up in the language or relating areas of the dominant hemisphere.

**Attention-Stretch:** The attention-stretch is the time between consecutive switch-offs. A child's attention-stretch should be long enough to cope with the longest sub-task given by the teacher.

**Cerebellum:** The cerebellum is situated behind the brain-stem and part of its concern is with muscle co-ordination.

**Concentration:** 1. Concentration in its generally understood sense is the ability to pay attention to some thing, idea or person: a child is said to have poor concentration when his ability to attend is not as good as someone thinks it should be. 2. In this book, concentration is also conceived as an entity which not only gathers on the language side of the brain to form attention, but which also moves voluntarily or involuntarily to the creative side of the brain and to the brain-stem. This concept of concentration allows us to think of 'concentration-flow'.

**Concentration-Flow:** Concentration-flow refers to the idea of concentration moving at a switch-off rest pause, and to the representation of such movement on a flowchart, such as Figure 1.

**Crawling:** The English 'crawl'/American 'creep' refers to moving forward on hands and knees. The hand and opposite knee come forward together in a cross-pattern movement. The American 'crawl' /English 'wriggle' refers to the child dragging his body along the floor in various ways. The terms sitting-crawl and cross-crawl refer to exercises.

*Dominance:* Dominance in this book is the same as hemispheric dominance, sometimes referred to as cerebral dominance, although the term hemispheric dominance is more accurate. It refers to one hemisphere being in overall control of language and movement, even when a motor control area is in the opposing hemisphere. Nearly all right-handers and most left-handers have language in the left hemisphere, which is the case considered in this book. However, the right hand is always controlled by the left motor area of the brain, and vice versa.

*Dyslexia and Specific Learning Difficulties:* At present, the terms dyslexia and specific learning difficulties are usually regarded as interchangeable. However, dyslexia implies a particular cause which, as yet, is not agreed upon, and the latter term is preferred in education.

*Homolateral Position:* In the homolateral position, the arm and leg on one side of the body are forward while the opposite arm and leg are to the rear. An example is the recovery position shown in Figures 7 & 12.

*Learning and Learning Difficulties:* The terms 'learning' and 'learning difficulties' in this book refer to those normally found in mainstream education unless otherwise stated.

*Myelination:* Myelination refers to the insulation of nerve pathways. It is required, for example, when a dominant language side of the brain is forming.

*Physical Basis of Concentration:* This term refers to a basis for establishing and maintaining concentration on the language side of the brain by physical means as far as this is possible. Although 'physical' in the title could be replaced by physiological or, more precisely, neuro-physiological, the means considered are simply physical.

*Pons:*  The pons (meaning 'bridge') is the part of the brain-stem connecting with the cerebellum.

*Sidedness:*  Language is associated with the language areas of the brain and is more effective if it becomes dominant in one hemisphere, giving rise to 'hemispheric dominance', which occurs in the child at an average age of about eight years. Primarily, it commands hands, ears, eyes and feet, each of which is more effectively commanded when one side of the brain or the other is dominant for those functions; that is, when 'sidedness' has been established. It is even more helpful if all these functions are dominant in the language hemi sphere; that is, 'one-sidedness' has been established: language, hands, ears, eyes and feet chiefly stimulate one hemisphere and allow the other side to remain relatively quiet, offering minimum interference to the establishment of hemispheric dominance.

*Sleeping Position:*  The sleeping position (Figures 7 & 12) is the transformed tonic neck reflex position which is, basically, the recovery/relaxation/coma position shown in many first-aid books. A difference on cold nights between the sleeping position and the recovery position may be that the upper hand is low enough to be under cover like the ear.

*Sleeping-Turn:*  The child begins the sleeping-turn in the recovery position and rolls over on the chest into the same position on his other side. It may be learnt in five movements (Figures 7 to 12) before becoming one smooth movement. The 'Repeated Sleeping-Turn' is the stationary form of the homolateral wriggle.

*Sleeping Work /Routine:*  The sleeping work or routine is concerned with adequate rest to minimise switch-off rest pauses at school. It is based on the idea of sleeping or resting for 20 minutes or more in the recommended sleeping position.

| | |
|---|---|
| ***Specific*** <br> ***Learning*** <br> ***Difficulties:*** | The term specific learning difficulties (SpLD) replaces the term severe learning difficulties (SLD), which is now applied to the mentally handicapped. For the idea in this book, SpLD may (1) occur before a child achieves a late general dominance when difficulties are likely to be 'general' or (2) remain after he gains a general dominance when difficulties are 'specific' to an area, or areas, such as spelling. <br> It is suggested that SpLD may often be a combination of those learning difficulties which may be taught in normal fashion plus an excessive number of tiny switch-off rest pauses. |
| ***Switch-Off*** <br> ***Rest Pause*** <br> ***Error:*** | Unexpected little mistakes are considered to result mostly from switch-off rest pauses. These cause short periods of considerably lowered attention or concentration on the language/ relating side of the brain. One might refer to maintaining attention as keeping 'switched in'. |
| ***Task-Chunks:*** | Task-chunks or sub-tasks are small parts of a task which themselves can stand as a completed task. Each one one should be completed without a switch-off rest pause interrupting it and causing an error. |
| ***Upper Junior:*** | An upper junior is a child in Years 5 or 6, by which time a retained high variability of spelling should be a cause for concern. |
| ***Variability:*** | Variability refers, unless otherwise stated, to the average variability of spelling errors tested in double mini-dictations on at least three different days and normally on a minimum of 20 countable errors (see Appendix 5). |
| ***Words Side:*** | The language hemisphere is often referred to as the words side. The term is used so often that it has been considered neater to leave out the |

apostrophe, similarly with the 'pictures side', referring to the visuo-spatial hemisphere.

*Wriggling:* See Crawling.

*Year and Age:* A child is in Year 5, for example, if he begins the school year (September to July) having reached the age of 9 years.

# *Index*

# Crown House Publishing Limited

Crown Buildings,
Bancyfelin,
Carmarthen, Wales, UK, SA33 5ND.
Telephone: +44 (0) 1267 211345
Facsimile: +44 (0) 1267 211882
e-mail: bshine@crownhouse.co.uk
Website: www.crownhouse.co.uk

We trust you enjoyed this title from our range of bestselling books for professional and general readership. All our authors are professionals of many years' experience, and all are highly respected in their own field. We choose our books with care for their content and character, and for the value of their contribution of both new and updated material to their particular field. Here is a list of all our other publications.

**Change Management Excellence:** *Putting NLP To Work In The 21st Century*
by Martin Roberts PhD                                 Hardback                    £25.00

**Doing It With Pete:** *The Lighten Up Slimming Fun Book*
by Pete Cohen & Judith Verity                       Paperback                   £9.99

**Dreaming Realities:** *A Spiritual System To Create Inner Alignment Through Dreams*
by John Overdurf & Julie Silverthorn              Paperback                   £9.99

**Ericksonian Approaches:** *A Comprehensive Manual*
by Rubin Battino MS & Thomas L. South PhD      Hardback                    £29.50
                                                              Accompanying tape      £9.99

**Figuring Out People:** *Design Engineering With Meta-Programs*
by Bobby G. Bodenhamer DMin & L. Michael Hall PhD   Paperback           £12.99

**Gold Counselling, Second Edition:** *A Structured Psychotherapeutic Approach To The Mapping And Re-Aligning Of Belief Systems*
by Georges Philips & Lyn Buncher                  Paperback                   £16.99

**Grieve No More, Beloved:** *The Book Of Delight*
by Ormond McGill                                       Hardback                    £9.99

**Hypnotherapy Training:** *An Investigation Into The Development Of Clinical Hypnosis Training Post-1971*
by Shaun Brookhouse PhD                            Spiralbound                 £9.99

**Influencing With Integrity:** *Management Skills For Communication & Negotiation*
by Genie Z Laborde PhD                               Paperback                   £13.50

**Instant Relaxation:** *How To Reduce Stress At Work, At Home And In Your Daily Life*
by Debra Lederer & L. Michael Hall PhD           Paperback                   £8.99

**The Magic Of Mind Power:** *Awareness Techniques For The Creative Mind*
by Duncan McColl PhD                                 Paperback                   £8.99

**A Multiple Intelligences Road To An ELT Classroom**
by Michael Berman                                      Paperback                   £16.99

**Multiple Intelligences Poster Set**
by Jenny Maddern                                       Nine posters                £19.99

**The New Encyclopedia Of Stage Hypnotism**
by Ormond McGill — Hardback — £29.99

**Now It's YOUR Turn For Success!** *Training And Motivational Techniques For Direct Sales And Multi-Level Marketing*
by Richard Houghton & Janet Kelly — Paperback — £9.99

**Peace Of Mind Is A Piece Of Cake**
by Michael Mallows & Joseph Sinclair — Paperback — £8.99

**The POWER Process:** *An NLP Approach To Writing*
by Sid Jacobson & Dixie Elise Hickman — Paperback — £12.99

**Precision Therapy:** *A Professional Manual Of Fast And Effective Hypnoanalysis Techniques*
by Duncan McColl PhD — Paperback — £15.00

**Principled Headship:** *A Teacher's Guide To The Galaxy*
by Terry Mahoney — Paperback — £9.99

**Rapid Cognitive Therapy, Volume 1:** *The Professional Therapists' Guide To Rapid Change Work*
by Georges Philips & Terence Watts — Hardback — £20.00

**Scripts & Strategies In Hypnotherapy**
by Roger P. Allen — Hardback — £19.99

**The Secrets Of Magic:** *Communicational Excellence For The 21st Century*
by L. Michael Hall PhD — Paperback — £14.99

**Seeing The Unseen:** *A Past Life Revealed Through Hypnotic Regression*
by Ormond McGill — Paperback — £12.99

**Slimming With Pete:** *Taking The Weight Off Body AND Mind*
by Pete Cohen & Judith Verity — Paperback — £9.99

**Smoke-Free And No Buts!**
by Dr Geoff Ibbotson & Dr Ann Williamson — Paperback — £5.99

**Solution States:** *A Course In Solving Problems In Business With The Power Of NLP*
by Sid Jacobson — Paperback — £12.99

**The Sourcebook Of Magic:** *A Comprehensive Guide To NLP Techniques*
by L. Michael Hall PhD & Barbara Belnap — Paperback — £14.99

**The Spirit Of NLP:** *The Process, Meaning And Criteria For Mastering NLP*
by L. Michael Hall PhD — Paperback — £12.99

**Sporting Excellence:** *Optimising Sports Performance Using NLP*
by Ted Garratt — Paperback — £9.99

**Still – In The Storm:** *How To Manage Your Stress And Achieve Balance In Life*
by Dr Ann Williamson — Paperback — £5.99

**Time-Lining:** *Patterns For Adventuring In "Time"*
by Bobby G. Bodenhamer DMin & L. Michael Hall — Paperback — £14.99

**The User's Manual For The Brain:** *The Complete Manual For Neuro-Linguistic Programming Practitioner Certification*
by Bobby G. Bodenhamer DMin & L. Michael Hall PhD — Hardback — £29.50

**Vibrations For Health And Happiness:** *Everyone's Easy Guide To Stress-free Living*
by Tom Bolton — Paperback — £9.99

# Order form

| Qty | Title |
|---|---|
| — | Change Management Excellence |
| — | Doing it with Pete |
| — | Dreaming Realities |
| — | Ericksonian Approaches |
| — | Ericksonian Approaches tape |
| — | Figuring Out People |
| — | First Steps |
| — | Gold Counselling Second Edition |
| — | Grieve No More, Beloved |
| — | Hypnotherapy Training |
| — | Influencing With Integrity |
| — | Instant Relaxation |
| — | The Magic Of Mind Power |
| — | A Multiple Intelligences Road To An ELT Classroom |
| — | Multiple Intelligences Poster Set |
| — | New Encyclopedia Of Stage Hypnotism |
| — | Now It's YOUR Turn For Success! |

| Qty | Title |
|---|---|
| — | Peace Of Mind Is A Piece Of Cake |
| — | The POWER Process |
| — | Precision Therapy |
| — | Principled Headship |
| — | Rapid Cognitive Therapy |
| — | Scripts & Strategies In Hypnotherapy |
| — | The Secrets Of Magic |
| — | Seeing The Unseen |
| — | Slimming With Pete |
| — | Smoke-Free And No Buts! |
| — | Solution States |
| — | The Sourcebook Of Magic |
| — | The Spirit Of NLP |
| — | Sporting Excellence |
| — | Still – In The Storm |
| — | Time-Lining |
| — | The User's Manual For The Brain |
| — | Vibrations For Health And Happiness |

**Postage and packing**

UK:
£2.50 for one book
£4.50 for two or more books

Europe: £3.50 per book
Rest of the world £4.50 per book

## My details:

Name: Mr/Mrs/Ms/Other (please specify) ........................................................................................................

Address: ........................................................................................................

........................................................................................................

........................................................................................................

Postcode: ...........................................................Daytime tel: .....................................

I wish to pay by:

☐ Amex        ☐ Visa        ☐ Mastercard        ☐ Switch – Issue no./Start date:..........................

Card number:...........................................................Expiry date:..........................

Name on card: ...........................................................Signature: ..........................

☐ cheque/postal order payable to **AA Books**

### Please send me the following catalogues:

☐ Accelerated Learning (Teaching Resources)
☐ Accelerated Learning (Learning to learn)
☐ Neuro-Linguistic Programming
☐ NLP Video Library – hire (UK and Ireland only)
☐ NLP Video Library – sales
☐ Ericksonian Hypnotherapy
☐ Classical Hypnosis
☐ Gestalt Therapy

☐ Psychotherapy/Counselling
☐ Trainer's Resources
☐ Business
☐ Freud
☐ Jung
☐ Transactional Analysis
☐ Parenting
☐ Special Needs

Please fax/send to our distributors:
**The Anglo American Book Company Limited**
**FREEPOST SS1340**
**Crown Buildings, Bancyfelin,**
**Carmarthen, SA33 4ZZ,**
**United Kingdom.**
**Tel: +44 (0) 1267 211880  Fax: +44 (0) 1267 211882**
or e-mail your order to:
*books@anglo-american.co.uk*
*www.anglo-american.co.uk (secure ordering system)*